Advance Praise for Coming Home

A fundamental challenge for our time is the move to embrace communi[illegible] environment within the context of individual values. It is th[illegible] Charles and Samples have mapped as a gentle, ste[illegible]
Mary Catherine Bateson
Author of *Full Circles, Overlapping Lives* and *W*[illegible]

This inspiring and practical book puts the emphasis [illegible] on what each of us can do as individuals to make the [illegible] place. I learned a long time ago that the buck stops with me. This book [illegible]ngs that lesson home to each of us. Read it and put the ideas to work in your own life. Our communities will all be the better for it. Bravo, Cheryl and Bob.
Ann Richards
Former Governor, State of Texas

As an elected and appointed government official, I have met people throughout the world and from all walks of life. There is a deep yearning among us all to make our communities peaceful, healthy and safe for generations to come. Bob and Cheryl bring us great insight and common sense to help accomplish that goal.
Bill Richardson, Governor, State of New Mexico
Former Congressman, Former US Secretary of Energy,
and Former Ambassador to the United Nations

The message that Cheryl and Bob offer is critical to success. Culture is the only thing the competition can't copy. Having that sense of community separates the top tier of companies.
C. Webb Edwards, President, Wells Fargo Services Company
Executive Vice President, Wells Fargo & Company

Cheryl and Bob live the lives of personal responsibility and leadership for the common good. They know that strong communities start with personal commitments. As a Mayor, a Congressman, and a business leader, I know first hand the challenge of building strong communities through resolving conflicts, and I have seen personal responsibility change outcomes for the better.
Steve Bartlett, President and CEO, The Financial Services Roundtable
Former Congressman, State of Texas, and Former Mayor of Dallas

As public officials, we are seeing an increase in ethnic, economic, and other divisive factors in our communities. Coming Home *serves a critical role in helping us deal with these factors and move forward to building healthy, livable communities.*
Tom Udall, Member of Congress
US House of Representatives, State of New Mexico

Coming Home *is a field guide for the renewal of optimism. Charles and Samples offer a joyful celebration of their 30 year collaboration in search of the keys to healthy human communities. Drawing upon a deep knowledge and appreciation for the inherent harmony of natural systems, they invite each of us to join in mindful examination of who we are, how we fit, and how we can contribute to a new renaissance for the human spirit.*
Susan Munroe and Terry Smith
Entrepreneurs, Educators, Community Leaders

In a world preoccupied with terror, war and mutual distrust, Cheryl Charles and Bob Samples have paused to show us how we might "create a peaceful, healthy and sustainable future for generations to come." Thanks to this gentle and compelling book, we are able to imagine a far better world and—very important!—to take those first crucial steps toward making it happen. Charles and Samples believe that healthy communities begin with healthy individuals ("the environment within ourselves"), and that on this congenial base we can gather our creative forces to build ever larger and more effective communities. Long before the end of Coming Home, *we believe it, too.*
Gregory Curtis
Managing Director and Chairman of the Board, Greycourt and Co., Inc.
Founding Director, The Investment Fund for Foundations

This book, this bouquet of words, is extraordinary. It lifts first the body, then the mind and finally the spirit. What a blessing it is for those who choose to receive its grace. It brings balance to the heart, understanding to the intellect and beauty to the soul. What a gift!
Rolland Smith
Emmy Award Recipient, Television Journalist, and Author

My Keresan people have a story that this continent was originally home to the horse as well as many others. When the earth cataclysmically changed because of man's foolish disobedience, the horse and many of the original peoples were gone. In time, the horse would one day return to this land. After the horse's return to this land, many others from around the globe would follow. Welcome, Bob and Cheryl. You've found a way home and you've put together a useful manual many others can use to help them come home. It's a joy listening to the stories of your adventures, meeting the people you've met, and learning from all that you've experienced. This is an old story still being told. We still have a lot to learn, listening, one to another. God bless you both.
Larry Littlebird
Artist, Author, *Hunting Sacred, Everything Listens*

Like few others, Charles and Samples understand what it takes to create healthy communities, because they understand that the nature of this complex series of relationships is not something we fix by applying a patch from outside the system. As they point out, by cultivating the environment, we encourage it to surface from within so that it can continually create itself anew. Coming Home *is brilliant and quietly revolutionary.*
Ron Schultz, Executive Director, Social Entrepreneur Incubator
Volunteers of America, Los Angeles

Bob and Cheryl offer valuable insights into the factors that contribute to the health of communities. They realize that communities are formed by more than their geographic location. Geography is important, but much more is involved. They take us to a rich understanding of the many kinds of communities which affect us all and how we can each contribute to our shared wellbeing.
Gail Lyons, Broker Owner, Boulder Real Estate Services, Ltd.
Chair, International Operations Committee, National Association of Realtors

Cheryl and Bob have created magic. I was delighted at the ease and gracefulness of the reading, the inspiration of the quotes to ground the learnings, and the practical guides for individual learning and reflection. I will definitely be using this book—to quote from, to share with others, to believe and be hopeful. How well they note the intense and profound changes occurring and the loss of hope and often the ability to cope with the change. Coming Home *is a "workbook" and gives me hope for a better future.*
Rosemary Romero
Facilitator, Mediator, Trainer
President, Association for Conflict Resolution

While written in the context of creating successful communities,
Coming Home *is a thorough, thoughtful examination of the values, attitudes and skills that lead to individual creativity and fulfillment, as well as to the capacity to function as a contributing participant in the various communities to which one belongs—whether school, workplace, neighborhood or chatroom.*
Letitia Chambers, Business Leader and Educator
Trustee, Institute of American Indian Art

Global thinking has to be tempered with insight into our own communities.
Coming Home *sets the stage for us to develop a course of action to bring back the importance and value of healthy communities. I especially like the practical activities interspersed throughout the book—things we can do in our own lives to enrich our sense of community.*
Joseph Hesbrook, Ph.D.
Tribal Liaison, Federal Emergency Management Agency
Founder, Advocates for Indigenous Interests

Cheryl Charles and Bob Samples have long been pioneers on the leading edge of conceptualization, integration and scholarship in the emerging and converging disciplines that include environmental education, sustainability and healthy communities. Coming Home *is a brilliant work designed to support the reshaping of all our communities. It examines the notion of community from multiple perspectives and provides a pathway for empowerment to begin to build healthy communities from "the inside out." Cheryl and Bob successfully argue that the metamorphosis of the American Dream must be a coming home to the visions, aspirations and values that have been the hallmark of healthy communities across the ages. Powerful reflective exercises provide the reader a context for developing the necessary leadership, knowledge and skills to actively build this new civic imperative. If you want to consciously engage in healthy community building, then* Coming Home *is a must-have resource—one that you will read again and again to draw inspiration from and to help chart your pathway to creating a healthier, peaceful, and sustainable future for you and those members of your community.*
Keith A. Wheeler
Executive Director, Center for a Sustainable Future
Co-Founder, Foundation for Our Future

Cheryl and Bob have created a captivating and critically important contribution to the literature on culture and communities. Many of the suggestions and observations from their work are being used today in the financial services industry's collective work through BITS. The insights are as practical for business as they are for the non-profit and public sectors. Their emphasis on collaborative problem solving in competitive environments is especially useful for the corporate sector.
Catherine A. Allen
CEO, BITS,
A Non-Profit Consortium of the 100 Largest U.S. Financial Institutions

COMING HOME

Community, Creativity and Consciousness

Cheryl Charles
Bob Samples

Personhood Press
Fawnskin, California

Design and Photos by Cheryl Charles and Bob Samples.
Authors' photo by Steve Yadzinski.

Library of Congress Cataloging-in-Publication Data
available on request.

Personhood Press
PO Box 370
Fawnskin, California 92333
1-800-429-1192
personhoodpress@att.net
www.personhoodpress.com

Printed in the United States of America

First Printing, April 2004

COMING HOME

Community, Creativity and Consciousness

DEDICATION

Come dance with the west wind and touch on the mountaintops, sail o'er the canyons and up to the stars, and reach for the heavens and hope for the future, and all that we can be and not what we are.
John Denver
The Eagle and the Hawk

We dedicate this book to all the dreamers and doers
who are working, alone and with others,
to create a peaceful, healthy and sustainable future
for generations to come.

With Special Thanks to
Della and Milton McClaren
Beth and Charles Miller
Stician Marin Samples

TABLE OF CONTENTS

Foreword

The word community is one of those terms that is so widely used in modern parlance that its significance has been obscured, or its meaning taken for granted. In *Coming Home* Cheryl Charles and Bob Samples invite us to reinvest the word with meaning and to consider its importance in our daily lives and society in general.

Cheryl Charles and Bob Samples bring many perspectives to this reflection on community, but perhaps most important is their attempt to show the congruence between the ecology of non-human communities and human communities. Also important is the development of a set of clearly stated and developed principles for the development and maintenance of communities, combined with a number of activities, placed throughout the book as guides for reflection and means of synthesis for the reader. In a real sense, the principles outlined here provide the basis for developing a curriculum for community building and articulate an agenda for skill development by those who wish to seriously engage in it.

This book will be a useful addition to the libraries of those who are interested in community planning, public participation, and organizational development. I hope it will serve as a springboard for the development of educational and action programs focused on equipping communities for renewal and reinvention.

Milton McClaren, Ph.D.
Emeritus Professor of Education,
Simon Fraser University, Burnaby, British Columbia
Adjunct Professor, Organizational Leadership and Learning,
Royal Roads University, Victoria, B.C.

INTRODUCTION

These are turbulent times. There is so much suffering in the world. Terrorism brings fear and tragedy. Natural disasters uproot and kill. Human cruelty brings death, starvation and emotional scars. Divisions of wealth and access to resources continue to undermine confidence and escalate conflict. These are not new challenges. There are some powerful differences, however, in contrast with challenges in times past. The rate at which change is occurring, fueled by new technologies; the accumulating effects of those changes; and the force with which the news of those changes and their impact is brought to us through current communications media—this combination is bringing these changes and challenges into the view and consciousness of most people on Earth, every day. There is little respite, there is much to grieve and worry about, even as there is much to celebrate. There is good news in the midst of the suffering. People throughout the world are taking action—sometimes bold, sometimes quiet—to bring kindness and good works to life.

So what do we do? How do we create the remedies and viable possibilities for actions that will work to solve these enormous problems? How do we celebrate and perpetuate the actions that serve to nourish and heal? That is what this book is about.

We begin by establishing the context—that is, why is it important to be thinking about the health of communities? It is important because healthy communities are the foundation for peace in the world. They inspire and sustain, and make possible a future of promise for generations to come. While our experience is principally in the United States, many of these concepts are applicable to other settings.

Why is it important
to be thinking
about the health of communities?
Because healthy communities
are the foundation
for peace in the world.

Our purpose is to inform thinking about contemporary communities and to encourage ways of thinking that tend to result in peaceful, healthy and sustainable communities over time. Our bias is clear. We believe that the human vision has slipped far from nature and the natural systems that once embraced us. We have gotten used to describing our concerns and looking for solutions while leaving nature's successful models out of the discussion. This lack of intimacy with nature's guiding principles affects the health of communities at all levels—personally and collectively.

Creativity is essential as an element in fostering healthy communities, and creativity in turn depends upon consciousness. Consciousness is also the foundation for facilitating a multiplier effect in which a critical mass of people thinking creatively about the health of communities puts that creativity to work through their consciousness in service. The book is intended to affirm how the creative process can inform consciousness and in turn facilitate a new sense of community for the 21st century.

We don't pretend to have answers, but we do offer direction. These observations, insights and suggestions come out of our life's work and our shared commitment to creating a peaceful, healthy and sustainable future—now and for generations to come. It is a time for "coming home."

Cheryl Charles
Bob Samples
Santa Fe, New Mexico

How to Use This Book

We hope that you will make this book a personal friend, that it will invite you to think about things you care about, to learn things about yourself in new ways, to be inspired to take actions that will serve you and all around you. We hope that reading the book and interacting with its concepts will be like time spent with a nourishing companion in conversation and exploration, support and encouragement. We hope it will inspire the dreamer in you, and support the doer in you. We hope it is among the voices that brings you to a new peace and balance in your life—at home with yourself, at home in your surroundings, at home with others, at home with the work we all must do to keep the world at peace for generations to come. We wrote long ago, "Earth Is Home to Us All—Share It Responsibly." We still believe it, and we cherish the notion that it takes many of us to engage in the process of "coming home" before it will work for the whole.

We have written the book with the intent that any reader could pick it up, read for a while, make some notes, try some things, and come back to it over and over. Read it through once, taking the time to use your journal, to take breaks for yourself, and to reflect on what is changing in your life. Think about the conversation the voices in this book bring to you in your life, as a form of ongoing, highly personal, dialogue.

Once you have experienced the whole of the book, we hope you will return to it again and again—reading your notes, trying activities again, talking with others about the ideas, and putting the concepts to work in your life. Think of it as a personal notebook, a resource that can grow and change with you over time.

Both of us are note-takers when we read. We long ago got over the stigma that it was somehow wrong to mark the pages of a book with our own notes and comments. In fact, we've decided that underlining, turning down pages, writing notes in the margins, and making sketches along the way are all ways to help us make a book a friend. It becomes easy to come back to an idea, to remember our initial response, to reinforce the idea and our interactions with it, to make it our own in that it integrates with our own consciousness. Leaving a visual trail is a way to serve the heart and the mind.

So you will find a lot of white space in these pages. Part of that is tied to our own sense of the aesthetic. Another part has to do with our commitment to learning. Leaving white space allows for sketches and notes that you can write along the way, and find again with ease, because the space encourages that process.

In addition to feeling comfortable writing within the pages of this book, making it a collaborative process as you interact with it, and, by extension, with us, we hope you will also keep a personal journal—one of those bound books with blank pages on which you can write, draw, paste artifacts, and explore even more in the privacy of your own journal's environment.

You will find that we suggest numerous activities along the way. We suggest, in addition to writing on the pages, that you use a journal throughout the process of reading this book. Ideally, this would be a journal that you begin just as you start the book, and that you keep solely for the purpose of your notes, observations and insights. If you take that approach, you will end up with two tangible records of your experiences—what you include in your journal, and what our book becomes in your hands as you personalize it.

Each section of the book begins with a quote—often by someone we know, who has inspired us, likely mentored us at times in our lives, and is a friend both personally and in our shared commitment to ideas that matter. We typically define a few terms, using standard references, as a way to establish some context for the major concepts each chapter is exploring. We set the stage for why we think a set of ideas is important. We provide our perspective so you have a sense of what we have learned and think is meaningful about a subject. We include suggested activities, so that you can take a few minutes or longer to do something with the ideas—to stretch, interact with others, and document your own insights to learn from at the moment, and reflect on later as well. We encourage you to use your journal. We encourage you to get outside, in the living world, as a physical way to reconnect with what we have always called "the first classroom." And throughout, we encourage you to take or leave what you find, to agree or disagree. Make this experience your own.

PART ONE

THE CONTEXT

> *Each of the memories I have picked up along the way represents an encounter with a place and a time that goes beyond the particular but might have been invisible without the contrasts of strangeness, for one is forced by cultural difference to question assumptions and struggle for active understanding.*
>
> Mary Catherine Bateson
> *Peripheral Visions: Learning Along the Way*

We live in times of extraordinary change, immersed in oceans of information, with immense mobility, technological tools and access to resources. At the same time, the gap between those of the greatest financial resources and wealth and those of the least is raising tensions and debate throughout the world.

What is needed is a whole view of the characteristics of healthy communities and a greater awareness of those processes that can be employed to facilitate the health of communities. Communities need people with the skills and conviction to assist in developing leadership, practicing collaboration, and achieving peaceful results. Those attributes exist within each of us, and can be nourished among us all.

We begin with a belief that there is a need to disseminate information about the characteristics of healthy communities and processes for achieving them. We believe that with such information, encouragement to practice the arts of community building, and the inspiration that comes from personal experience, people throughout the world can put the ideas to work, in their own ways.

For our purposes in this book, healthy communities have many attributes, which we describe in detail in the chapters that follow. Healthy communities are cultural and natural systems where life and learning are nourished and the actions of members enable a peaceful and sustainable future. A healthy community functions by the laws of both culture and nature. Healthy communities embrace the integrity of choice and change while honoring the need for continuity and wholeness.

Healthy communities are
cultural and natural systems
where life and learning are nourished
and the actions of members
enable a peaceful and sustainable future.

The Patterns that Connect

It was Mary Catherine Bateson's father, Gregory Bateson, who said "context is a pattern through time." The context within which we live in the world today is unlike any other, and yet it is rich in pattern. To make sense of these times, we need to be discerning. We need to be able to read the patterns. We need to be able to see the strange in the familiar, and the familiar in the strange. This form of recognizing patterns, and changes in the relationships within patterns, is fundamental to the creative process. Reading the patterns will inform our thinking, and help to give us the skills, insights, and experiences that will help us—each of us—contribute to the health of environments, beginning within ourselves, in our relationships, and in our ways of being members of communities of all kinds.

Bateson claimed that, for us to recognize change, we have to see a difference in the relationships between the parts and the patterns that these relationships express. As the pattern varies in context, relationships can be detected.

In natural systems, patterns are expressed within the context of the overall characteristics of an ecosystem. Organisms live in relationship to others. Each individual organism has relationships with others of its own kind, and with a suite of different life forms. Patterns may change in response to changes in climate, disease, reproduction rates, food supplies and other characteristics of habitat, and the general balance of interactions among the parts of any ecosystem.

Context becomes the combined expression of patterns and relationships. Patterns govern the continuity of life systems. Relationships determine day-to-day interactions. Both are subject to change. Sometimes the environment imposes changes. Other times the change is born from within the self-regulating characteristics of life itself.

In natural systems, changes in patterns are most often emergent—that is, they are created from forces within the system rather than from outside influences. Emergent change accompanies the uninterrupted functioning of a system.

Humans often exercise another form of change—imposed change. Imposed change is directed at a system in an effort to alter or enhance its function.

Many of us today try to manage change and some of us think of ourselves as "change agents." We believe that we will be far more effective participants in any setting—family, business, community, and planetary—if we understand and appreciate both forms of change. We urge an approach that recognizes emergent change within the context of natural systems, and uses great restraint in exercising imposed change.

Organisms live within a specific kind of context—a habitat. For wildlife, suitable habitats are those environments in which food, water, shelter and space are effectively arranged in a pattern that is conducive to the species' survival. Habitats are patterns of living relationships. Some relationships are explicit, like when a bluebird eats an insect or a hawk eats a vole. Other relationships are more subtle, like the effects of changes in rainfall cycles and the timing of the sexual maturation of sea turtles. Organisms must fit within and participate in the process of creating patterns within habitats in order to survive. All life forms must adapt to changes in time—that is, in Bateson's terms—to adapt to the context of patterns through time. If relationships change, so do the patterns, and vice versa. With a change in pattern, we have a change in context. If we don't, as humans, pay attention to these changes—and our tendencies to affect them—there can be an accumulation of unintended consequences with sometimes disastrous results.

Here is an example of how things can go wrong as a result of imposed change.

We once watched a small family of mongooses forage in the shrubbery below a balcony at a resort hotel on the big island of Hawaii. Before mongooses were turned into tourists in the Hawaiian islands, they were native to India. Mongooses are successful creatures, resourceful in reproduction and adaptation. Living for centuries in India, they were known to kill and eat snakes. This attribute was appreciated by the Indian people. The colonizing British, observing the mongoose's affinity for killing and eating snakes, were also appreciative.

It was not long before some people decided that if mongooses killed snakes successfully in India, they could do so in other geographic settings. This is how the mongoose came to be what we humans might call a reluctant tourist. The mongoose fit appropriately within the context of its native environment in India, just as all native plants and animals fit appropriately within the context of their habitats throughout the world.

Unfortunately, in this case, a decision was made to take the mongoose to other places in the world in which the British had colonies. The British colonialists concluded that the fear of snakes held by many British citizens could be reduced by taking the snake-killing mongooses abroad and enlisting them in the Queen's service. And so, the mongoose began to travel the world under a British passport. One place the mongoose was introduced was Hawaii. The introduction of nonnative species is always a form of imposed change, and nearly always brings a host of unintended consequences. In this case, the results were compounded by the fact that Hawaii had never had snakes.

Parts of a context, when taken separately from the pattern in which they exist, tend not to transfer well. The mongoose was only a single element in a pattern that had developed over an extremely long period of time. This became evident when the mongoose began to adapt to its new environment. Mongooses, it seems, like to eat many things in addition to snakes—including eggs, young birds, small rodents, and insects. Opportunistic, as are most predators, the mongooses began eating a wide variety of eggs—chicken, duck, songbird and even turtle. The impact has been devastating—particularly on the native species.

Humans make decisions. To make them without understanding the context can have, as did the mongoose decision, wide-ranging and sometimes horrific consequences. Now, Hawaii's ecosystem is turned upside down. Species, once at home, are displaced and even made extinct.

Activity: Journaling and Soft Eyes

Throughout this book, we encourage the use of a personal journal for reflections and observations. One helpful approach comes from *The Artist's Way at Work,* by Mark Bryan, Julia Cameron and Catherine Allen. It encourages readers to write each morning—literally writing no more than three pages. It is a personally reflective and head-clearing way to start the day. The book also encourages "time-outs" of the sort where, once a week, you do something refreshing and pleasant for yourself, alone, just for you. We encourage both activities, remembering that healthy communities begin with healthy individuals—and that process begins by taking care of your self.

With that as an introduction, find yourself a bound book with blank pages—they are sold in bookstores, stationery stores, and a variety of other places. Pick one that pleases you in terms of touch, size, and overall aesthetic. Put your name and today's date in the book. Take a few minutes to write a one-page introduction—write about why you decided to read *Coming Home*, and what you hope to learn and accomplish as a result.

One way to begin to discern patterns begins with what we call "soft eyes and hard eyes." Go outside, with your journal in hand. Ideally, pick a place that you enjoy visually. Find a spot to stand in which you can see 180 degrees with ease. Take a few moments to scan from left to right, looking in detail at the environment and its contents. That process is looking with "hard eyes." Take your journal and write a few notes about what you see.

Now, do the same thing, but shift your vision so that you are looking at the big picture—that is, scan for the whole of what you are seeing and how it fits together. Forget about the detail and visually experience the whole of the setting, using the technique again of moving from left to right. This time you are using "soft eyes."

Write a few notes to yourself about the effect you experience. What are the characteristics of the view you see with soft eyes? With hard eyes? Are there differences? Similarities? Both skills are useful. We often see only the parts, and not the whole.

Complex Adaptive Systems

One of the sources of insight available to us is in the study of complex adaptive systems. Not yet a science, it is an emerging discipline. An interdisciplinary group of scientists and scholars from diverse fields has been working for the past decade to identify and understand the connections within systems of many different kinds—the patterns that connect—in whole and systemic ways in order to make predictions and understand phenomena more fully. In this case, technology has helped. Computing capacities are part of the process, especially when predictive software is applied to determine the characteristics of the complex adaptive systems.

Why does this matter? Because the work is fostering an awareness of the connections that exist among us all, and is generating insights about a variety of attributes of communities of all kinds. Concepts related to human behavior under stress, human resilience, accommodation to change and evolutionary tendencies are emerging with more clarity than has previously been the case as a result of the work in this field of study.

The Power of Metaphor

> *Metaphoric effectiveness ... is effective by connecting domains of experience that were before apart, but with the form of connectedness that has the discipline of art.*
>
> Jerome Bruner
>
> *On Knowing: Essays for the Left Hand*

The words we choose have more impact than we sometimes consider. We think about this in a variety of ways. One way has to do with what metaphors engender in our individual thinking, and within groups, including at social, political and cultural levels.

At the most specific level, we have found that organic, biological, natural systems metaphors have inherent the capacity to stimulate generative thinking. They tend to nourish creativity. Mechanical, nonliving metaphors have the opposite effect. They are controlling, limiting and nongenerative. "Circle the wagons" has one effect. "Life is an eddy in the water's flow" has another.

In recent times, what we call the "Newtonian paradigm" has had a disproportionate impact on the metaphors we choose, and therefore the ways in which we think.

It goes like this. Newton made it easy for us to call upon the workings of gears, clocks, switches, and levers to communicate how we interact with the world. This multiplied to the tools of war, and those of the Internet environment. Highly desirable results are often described as "working like clockwork" or "driving the engines of war." We say we "flipped the switch" as we move to a new perspective. We report that we "applied leverage" when we gained a competitive advantage. "Light bulbs going on," "finely meshed gears," "keeping things on the back burner," and a "perfectly tuned engine" have come to represent how our minds work. Failure is characterized by concepts such as "a wrench in the works," "short circuits," and "blown fuses." The human mind is a computer; our planetary home is Spaceship Earth.

These and many other mechanical metaphors have become common in the vocabulary we use to describe the world. As innocent as these words may seem, they carry the seeds of limitation embedded in our ways of thinking. Mechanical metaphors require a source of external energy. They depend on maintenance from outside sources. Clocks do not wind themselves, computers need electricity or some other power source, a spaceship needs mechanics and fuel, and weapons of war need instructions in order to be deployed.

Mechanical ways of thinking promote mechanical approaches to solving problems—whether one is thinking about oneself, relationships with others, participation in institutions, or conflicts in the global environment. When issues arise, we look for bigger hammers and more powerful weapons.

Biological metaphors, in contrast, have inherent within them the capacity for life. They are regenerative, and they do not require external intervention from humans, nor external maintenance as do machines. Biological metaphors tend to be healing. They are nourishing, made of the stuff of life itself.

Biological metaphors are alive. They hold the power to self-regulate. Mechanical metaphors are dead. They require external force and energy in order to have any effect.

Here are two contrasting uses of metaphor. Both represent a woman leader. The first is: *She was a lion in the meeting.* She exhibited strength, quickness, and a carnivore's capacity to move with speed. Female lions are killers and also attentive mothers. A number of other attributes may come to mind—resourcefulness, power, beauty. In contrast, consider this: *She was a bulldozer in the meeting.* Gone are the images of the cunning hunter with lithe maneuverability. In their place is a vision of a hulking machine that destroys whatever is in its path. The woman as bulldozer is a machine. Her power is tied to how much fuel remains in her tanks. The metaphor is inherently limited. Machines have no life.

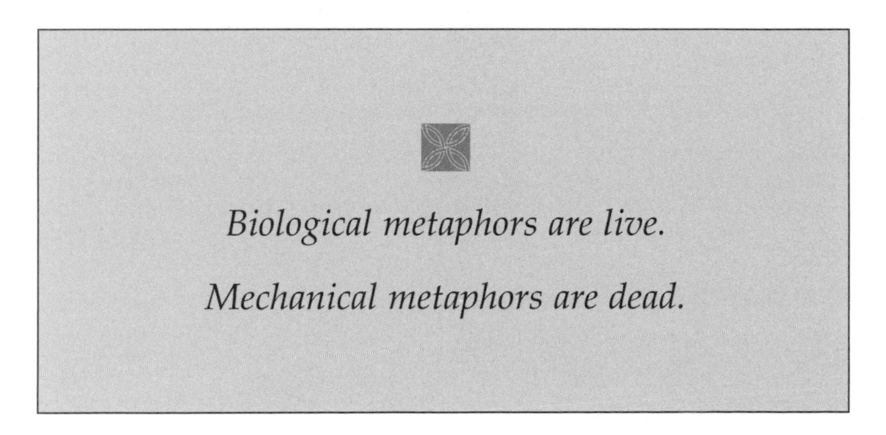

Biological metaphors are live.

Mechanical metaphors are dead.

Here is a comparison of some of the dominant characteristics of each type of metaphor.

MECHANICAL	NATURAL SYSTEMS
Nonorganic	*Organic*
Inanimate	*Animate*
Nonliving	*Living*
Static	*Dynamic*
Nonrenewable	*Renewable*
Nongenerative	*Generative*
Externally powered	*Internally powered*
Externally regulated	*Self regulated*
Limited options	*Numerous options*
Finite	*Infinite*

The results of a long-term study at Harvard University were reported in the 1960s by Robert Burden. The researchers found that students from rural areas in the United States were much more likely to use natural systems metaphors than were their urban counterparts. The speech of the rural students was rich with the generative metaphors of life and living things—the stuff of nature. Not surprisingly, farther from daily interactions with broad horizons of living landscapes, the urban students used metaphors and their close cousin, similes, drawn from machines and the built environment. Rural students would say, "quick as a fox," or "slow as maple syrup." Urban students would say, "slow as a quarter horsepower outboard motor," or "quick as Western Union."

Burden and his colleagues discovered that the students whose metaphors were derived from the living world consistently generated the most creative thinking during problem solving. Natural metaphors generated the most unique solutions to problems. This perspective influenced the development of Synectics by W.J.J. Gordon and George Prince in the early 1960s. Synectics remains one of the most original and productive approaches to creative problem solving. This is due in part to its recognition of the power of metaphor to influence consciousness, including creative capacities.

The metaphors we choose and use are the lifeblood of our worldview. They carry the meaning beyond the meaning. In a real sense, what is at stake is the freedom of the human mind. If I perceive the world as a machine, I will respond to it accordingly. I will either see it controlling me, or I will try to control it. In either case, I will be victim or master. If I perceive the environment in which I exist as alive, I am stepping into an open system with the capacity for continuing life. I have many more options if I choose the living world as my source of inspiration and the medium through which I choose to communicate. Metaphors are our medium. They influence who we are, how we think, and the ways in which we affect all others. Metaphors matter.

Metaphors influence who we are, how we think, and the ways in which we affect others.

Activity: My Metaphors

Use your journal to keep track of all the metaphors you use during a one-hour period. Keep a list in two columns—one for biological/natural systems metaphors and the other for cultural/mechanical metaphors.

Check the tendency to use one kind of metaphor more than another. Reflect on your results within your journal. Which do you tend to use most?

Write a page of observations in your journal about the differences in the effectiveness of the metaphors you choose.

If you found that you used no metaphors in that one-hour period, make a change. In your next conversation, try using a few of each kind of metaphor. Then reflect on and write about the results.

The Compelling Need

In order to survive, a plurality of true communities would require not egalitarianism and tolerance but knowledge, an understanding of the necessity of local differences, and respect. Respect, I think, always implies imagination—the ability to see one another, across our inevitable differences, as living souls.

Wendell Berry
The Art of the Common Place

These times demand imagination and innovation. The innovation must be grounded within the context of the times in which we live. We need to be able to read patterns, and to respect the distinctions between imposed and emergent change. Creativity is needed, in a spirit of collaboration, with a commitment to constructive change. If not, more heartache, tragedy, pain and suffering—with accumulating devastation to the life support systems of the planet itself—will be the result. With creativity, in a climate of informed and conscious choice, the world can be safer, saner, and healthier.

We have thought about where this creativity can make the most constructive difference, where it makes sense to focus our collective energies, beginning within each of us as individuals. Our answer is within the context of communities. We each live in communities of many kinds today.

Communities have both social and natural systems definitions. To ensure a peaceful, healthy and sustainable future, we think that our work can most fruitfully begin with the many communities in which we live, love, learn, work, wonder and play. We think it is time for "coming home." Communities are home to us all.

Activity: Communi-Me

On a page in your journal, list the communities within which you live, work, play and learn. Put a star by any to which you feel an especially strong affiliation or connection.

Make a second list of communities with which you believe you should have a connection, but in which you don't feel you actively participate. It is okay if some communities are on both lists.

Save these lists in your journal to refer to after we spend more time on the concept of community and its many forms in our lives.

People today are searching for meaning.
We lack a sense of the common good.
We struggle without recognizing the need
for civic virtue on a small planet.

PART TWO

COMMUNITY

Your heart to mine, my heart to yours,
talk about opening windows, talk about opening doors.
My heart to yours, your heart to mine,
love is the light that shines from heart to heart.
John Denver
Heart to Heart

com mu' ni ty, noun. a body of people having common organization or interests or living in the same place under the same laws; an assemblage of animals and plants living in a common home under similar conditions.

People today are searching for meaning. There is a loss of a sense of shared identity. People yearn for significant connections with others, while at the same time they struggle with a need for privacy and autonomy. Our nation's roots are founded in respect for diversity and yet we see great divisions and strife within parts of our country, our cities, the rural reaches, and our neighborhoods over issues of balancing diversity with wholeness. The same issues are played out and intensified in the global environment. We lack a sense of the common good—and, even when we identify it, we tend to lack the skills to achieve it. We struggle without recognizing the need for civic virtue on a small planet.

The foundations of responsible citizenship are at risk. Freedom is in peril. The characteristics of contemporary society have allowed us to separate and isolate without counterbalancing experiences to create a functioning whole out of the parts. Generational differences are in the mix as well. Many children and youth are feeling—and demonstrating—the breakdown of community health. As they lose faith, the principles of democracy are undermined.

Learners of all ages need knowledge, skills, attitudes, experiences and commitment to enable us to live as a community of the whole. We need to reinvigorate a sense of community, grounded in the basics of democratic practice. We need to rekindle confidence in the efficacy of individuals who demonstrate internal, rather than external, responsibility for outcomes in their lives. We need to understand how to live as individuals among others, in communities of communities, with enough sense of a shared meaning in life to prevent our differences from overwhelming our commonality. There is a profound need to reestablish the importance of civic literacy and to bring it to life within people throughout society. The arts of democracy cannot be taken for granted. To the extent that communities are dysfunctional, democracy is at risk.

Despite all the signs of stress and breakdown, we believe strongly in the will and capacity of individual citizens. We believe that a healthy society begins with self-governing individuals who take responsibility for their actions. We believe that the increasingly complex problems facing the United States and the world as a whole, and its communities, must be addressed by the informed and skilled participation of individuals—beginning in their homes, their neighborhoods, local organizations, businesses and municipalities.

We believe that what is needed today is a recommitment to civic literacy through a process of shared responsibility for results. In order to recommit to the foundational values of a democratic society, people of all ages need to renew, develop and improve their skills for resolving complex problems. We, as communities and nations, need a commitment to achieving a common good without sacrificing individual rights and freedoms. This is ever more important within the context of a world community in which some of these values are shared, and some are not.

We believe that a healthy society begins with self-governing individuals who take responsibility for their actions.

We begin our look at communities with those of humans, in a cultural context. We offer some characteristics of human communities, and identify those attributes that tend to indicate capacities for sustainability and health through time. We move from the cultural context to the first communities, those of the living world upon which all life depends. We establish an understanding of the characteristics of natural, enduring systems of life. Rather than anthropomorphizing—in which the characteristics of humans are brought to the nonhuman world—we naturomorphize, and draw insights from living systems to apply to human ecologies.

What Is Community?

The essence of community, its very heart and soul, is the non-monetary exchange of value; things we do and share because we care for others, and for the good of the place ... It arises from a deep, intuitive, often subconscious understanding that self-interest is inseparably connected with community interest.

Dee Hock
Birth of the Chaordic Age

We are often asked, "What do you mean by community?" Interestingly, the question follows what frequently appears as a physical response to the word—a look of palpable resonance, a visible quickening, an intake of breath and a smile. And then comes the question, "What do you mean by community?"

We define community broadly, flexibly, and yet with rigor. How can we do this simultaneously? By drawing from our commitment to the concept of community and humanity's current context.

We believe that there are many kinds of communities on many scales.

We believe that:

- Community requires a perception of belonging and supports a sense of identity.
- Community puts identity in context.
- Community requires participation and commitment.
- People can be members of many communities at the same time.
- The community provides support to individuals and every individual contributes to the community overall.
- Community in its optimal form is a coherent system that operates with all of its parts working effectively as individual self-contained elements and as a whole.
- Communities exercise a form of synergy—a coherent whole is created by more than a simple sum of the parts.

We define community as a dynamic set of relationships in which a synergic, self-regulating whole is created out of the combination of individual parts into a cohesive, identifiable, unified form.

Some communities may be defined geographically. Others are felt, such as in the expression, "a sense of community." Increasingly, communities are chosen, and transcend physical geography. The privilege of feeling "at home" in a community is tied to perception.

Community: a dynamic set of relationships in which a synergic, self-regulating whole is created out of the combination of individual parts into a cohesive, identifiable, unified form.

Activity:
Characteristics of Healthy Communities

Visualize a healthy community, one in which you feel safe and at home. Take a few art materials, and, in your journal, illustrate your healthy community, thinking consciously in the process about the elements you include.

Write a few paragraphs about how you feel in this healthy community and why it is important to you.

Now list the elements you think are essential to the health of this community. List those you think are essential, in some significant way, to the health of any community.

Imagine what it will take to create and sustain more communities of health, for more people, over time.

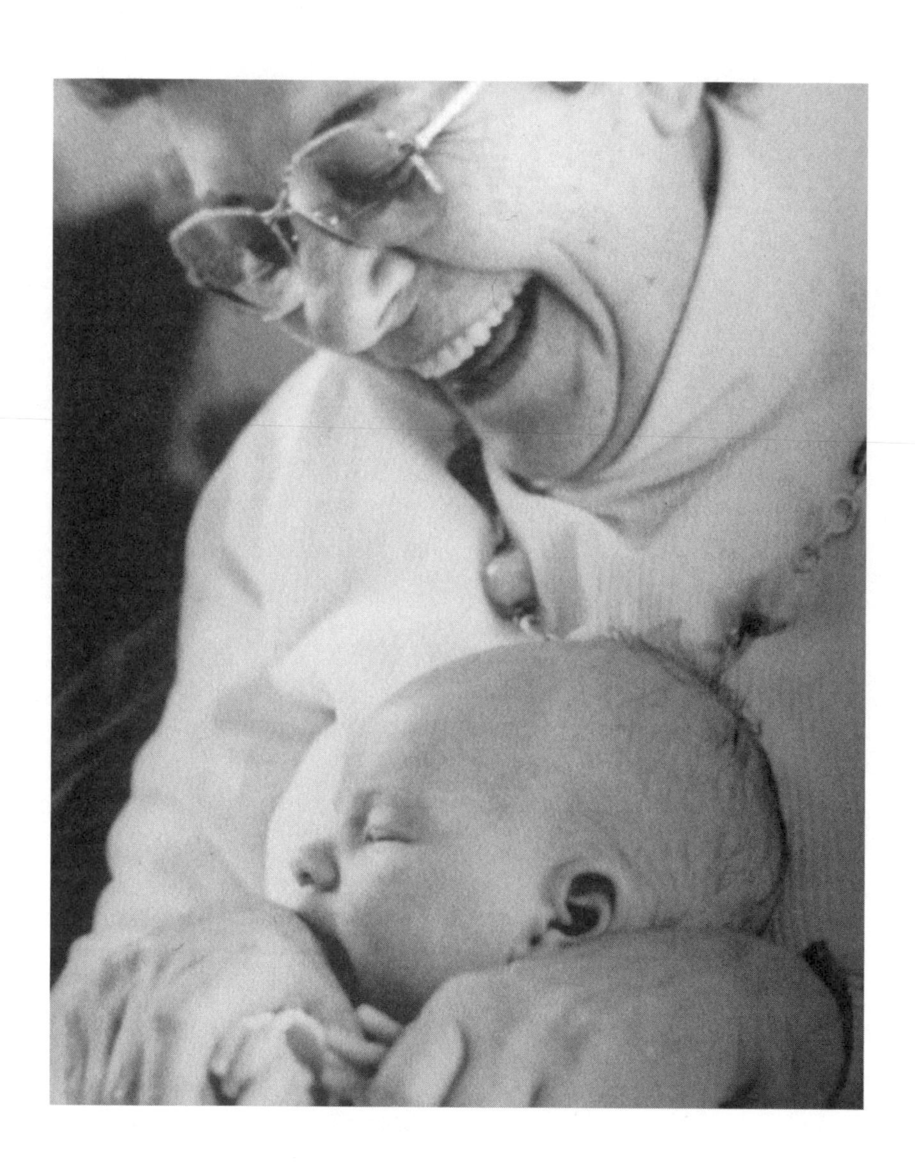

Characteristics of Human Communities

The traditional community could boast generations of history and continuity. Only a few communities today can hope to enjoy any such heritage. The rest, if they are vital, continuously rebuild their shared culture and consciously foster the norms and values that will ensure their continued integrity.

John W. Gardner
Building Community

Here are some of the characteristics of human communities. We distilled these through our explorations, especially during the period of time in which we co-founded the Center for the Study of Community with Beth and Charles Miller. Beth and Charles have a deep interest in community and demonstrate that in their many good works. John W. Gardner was also among those who most affected our thinking about these characteristics. We credit Beth, Charles and John for their insights, encouragement and convictions.

Sense of Shared Purpose

For a community of any size to function as a coherent whole, there must be a sense of shared purpose among most of its members. While it is possible for a community to function without all of its members being able to state and agree to this shared purpose, under optimal conditions most will be able to do so.

Agreement on Core Values

Tied to a sense of shared purpose is agreement on core values. Members of a community agree on at least a few major values.

Participation

Communities require participation. In order to share a sense of purpose and agree on core values, people must participate in the communities to which they belong. Some forms of participation are more active than others. Reflection can be a form of participation.

Communication

People need to communicate with other members of their communities in order, in part, to recognize that they are members of a community. They need to receive and to give communications. Such communication is a form of participation and helps to solidify a sense of shared purpose and agreement on shared values.

Commitment

Communities depend on their members' commitment to the community's health. Members of communities need to be committed to supporting the processes of community building that underlie healthy communities. People need to be committed to supporting whatever shared purposes are valued by the community as a whole. Commitment does not mean blind agreement. It means willingness to participate in the process of community building that underlies healthy communities over time.

Conscious Choice

Communities depend on their members being thoughtful about their shared purposes and common values, and, individually and collectively, actively choosing to exercise those responsibilities.

Shared Responsibility

Members of communities perceive and fulfill a sense of responsibility for the health and well-being of the community.

Equity

Healthy communities are characterized by equitable access to opportunities for influence, decision making and responsibility.

Openness

Whereas communities are characterized by shared values, the process of agreeing on shared values is dynamic and changing. Otherwise, people are inculcated in the operating values without taking personal responsibility for them. Openness to new ideas may result in changing values within communities. Communities that are closed to new ideas may find themselves with members who have internalized values without believing in them. Over time, such closed communities will die.

Respect for Differences

Related to openness is the dimension of respect for differences. People can disagree with one another and still be members of the same community. Without respect for differences, there is little room for openness to change. Further, different perspectives and experiences hold the possibility for enriching communities.

Acceptance

While members of communities may hold many differences, and disagreements may occur, communities are characterized by an acceptance of the inherent value of every person in them. Everyone has a role and potential contributions to make. Acceptance is about respect, not necessarily agreement.

Trust

People need to believe that certain agreements will be upheld, that common values will be respected within a fabric of accountability. Without trust, communities cannot exist.

Collaboration

Members of communities must work with others at least some of the time in order to accomplish tasks.

Reciprocity

There is exchange within communities. That is, people do things for one another and also have things done for them.

Accountability

Communities foster a self-regulating approach to being accountable for individual and group actions. Accountability is essential for maintaining community cohesion.

Efficacy

Members must be able to accomplish tasks of meaning and worth, and to perceive some sense of their value.

Perceived Skill

Members must be able to perceive that they are able to accomplish tasks of meaning and worth.

Cohesion

Communities are coherent—they take individuals, and groups of individuals, and coalesce them into an effective whole. The strongest communities are those that respect differences and similarities, learn from both, and simultaneously create a coherent whole out of what may be disparate parts in order to accomplish something for the common good.

Activity: More About Characteristics of Healthy Communities

Look back in your journal at your illustration of a healthy community and the previous activities you completed concerning the attributes of communities.

Think about what is missing from your images and lists. Wonder about what might bring the greatest humor, vitality, integrity, hope and consideration to any community you cherish.

Write a short list of possible “bumper stickers” to get the point across. Here is one of ours: Communities Matter—Start At Home Today.

Try a few of these slogans at home on the refrigerator door. Then, try one on your car bumper—and see how you feel.

Ways to Build and Sustain Healthy Communities

> *We cannot recreate the world of the frontier, even if we thought we wanted to. But there is something to be learned from the subtle but persistent process by which frontier families learned the politics of cooperation. They learned it the way almost anything worthwhile is learned—by practice.*
>
> Daniel Kemmis
>
> *Community and the Politics of Place*

With these characteristics of healthy communities in mind, there are ways in which to build and sustain the health of communities over time. Below are some of those we find to be enduring.

Sharing Stories, Traditions and Rituals

A sense of shared story has been at the heart of healthy communities through generations. The use of story in cultures is one of the oldest ways to build community, by supporting the individual's sense of identity within a context. Stories are missing today from people's daily lives. Or, the stories people hear come in fragments without coherence or the durability of time. Story is one of the most basic community-building techniques. Rituals and traditions are ways to create ceremony and substance around a community's values and can be used to reinforce the key teachings of any story.

Part of the value is repetition; part has to do with a feeling of specialness that surrounds the process. Rituals and traditions today take many forms, from football watching among some groups of friends to religious services to political conventions. Rituals are lost and traditions often lack authenticity in our contemporary, complex society. Many stories are being lost as well. Creating and participating in rituals, sustaining traditions, and protecting and perpetuating stories, are important community-building techniques.

Creating a Shared Vision

When beginning a community from scratch, a process for creating a shared vision is essential. When a community already exists, there must be a process for continually invigorating the vision, making sure it is understood and felt important by most members. Techniques for creating or recognizing or re-authenticating a shared vision are important skills.

Identifying and Agreeing on Core Values

One of the first steps in the process of creating a shared vision is to identify and agree on core, underlying values. Ways to do so can be taught and shared.

Creating Tangible Ways to Contribute and Participate

One of the most effective community-building techniques is authentic participation in something perceived to be of value. Doing so doesn't typically happen by chance, particularly as communities grow in size and complexity. Paying attention to how to create opportunities for involvement, and learning how to do so in a variety of settings and circumstances, are additional critical community-building skills.

Acknowledging Participation

There are diverse ways to acknowledge and affirm the participation of members of a community. They range from listening to giving awards. In every instance, to be effective, they must be authentic. Processes for effectively acknowledging participation can be taught.

Identifying Success and Failure

This is one dimension of monitoring progress against goals and objectives. It is a way to discern whether or not something is happening. Both success and failure are valuable. The key is to know the difference. Experience helps; skills can be taught.

Evaluating Progress

More complex than simply identifying success and failure, there are many ways to evaluate whether progress is being made within the context of building and sustaining healthy communities. Approaches to evaluating progress are demonstrable, teachable, replicable and measurable.

Learning How to Disagree and Agree

Particularly because of the growing confusion about shared values and a common vision within communities and among groups within communities, there is a critical need to teach people skills for differing and agreeing with one another in constructive ways. Mediation and conflict resolution are examples of processes that can assist in getting past disagreement to agreement.

Learning Skills of Collaboration

Whereas differences and disagreements can be healthy and constructive, it is critical that we teach people how to work together to accomplish mutually desired goals. Formal schooling in this society does little to prepare people for collaborative problem solving. These skills can be taught to learners of any age, with powerful benefits to individuals, groups and communities of many sizes and kinds.

Caring for Children

No society will endure with grace that does not care for its children. Societies comprise communities of many kinds and scales. To the extent that some communities do not care for children effectively, all communities in a society are affected. Whether or not individuals personally take responsibility for caretaking of children, all members of communities share to some extent in that extended responsibility. As a result, techniques for ensuring that children are cared for, and approaches for doing so, are essential parts of any program to nourish and sustain healthy communities.

Creating Intergenerational Learning

Just as children are the key to the long-term health of any community, learners of all ages must be cherished and supported. One of the most effective ways to sustain healthy communities depends on intergenerational learning, when, for example, long-living people spend time with children.

Developing Leadership and Responsibility in Members

Healthy communities recognize the leadership capacities within each individual and group. They nurture responsibility in everyone. Skills for doing so can be made explicit and taught.

Practicing Skills of Communication

Most community-building techniques depend upon effective skills of communication. Practice is one way to develop such skills.

Learning Techniques for Creating Cohesion

Creating wholeness out of differences is the principal challenge of community building. It depends on skills of communication, grounded in knowledge, and inspired by commitment. Many such techniques can be practiced and put to work in diverse settings.

Valuing Differences

With a goal of creating and sustaining communities, people sometimes forget the richness and importance of different perspectives. Resistance, defensiveness, and violence at the extreme can be the results of inadequate appreciation for differences. Processes for valuing differences can be taught and learned, practiced and improved.

Respecting the Need for the Common Good

Balancing respect for differences within a commitment to a larger, common good is an intellectual, emotional and practical challenge. Skills for achieving this goal can be taught.

Valuing Learning

Since change is a constant in all communities, one of the most important ways to live with change is to value learning. People sometimes forget their capacities to learn, and lose a willingness to do so. Characteristics of the learning process can be taught, and in turn serve as a foundation for community building.

Imagining the Future

Looking ahead with a reason—this is basic to successful communities. Ways to imagine the future can be taught and developed. Tied to all of the other community-building techniques, these skills are important to creating and sustaining healthy communities over time.

These characteristics of healthy communities and strategies for building community can be incorporated into the fabric of community life in many different ways. For example, those we call "leaders who are willing learners" can consciously cultivate, practice and teach one another how to do so—in families, schools, businesses, civic settings, churches, municipalities, and regions. The whole community-building movement in the United States in the last few decades is an example of a conscious commitment to doing so. As more and more parts of any society incorporate and practice the arts of community building, communities of communities will combine to help create a peaceful and healthy whole. The patterns will connect in a form of consciousness that transforms the world.

Some of the challenges we face include:

Multiplying and developing skills in depth. We need more people who can exercise a core set of community-building skills. Each of us has relevant skills, some more developed than others. We need a wider range of skills, less superficially and more consciously, among and within more people who in turn share a commitment to using those skills for the good of the whole.

Seeing the whole as well as the parts. As a society, we are increasingly good at fragmenting, polarizing and undermining the strengths of diversity. We are less adept at standing back and seeing—envisioning—a large view where the parts of any community fit together harmoniously and coherently. As a result, greater attention is needed to develop the skills for seeing and achieving a big picture while recognizing and cherishing the value of the individual parts.

Applying skills of collaboration. Having a range of community-building skills, including valuing the whole as well as the parts, is essential. It is also not enough. People need to be willing to act on the belief that collaboration is important in order to achieve a common good that serves most people responsibly most of the time.

Practicing commitment. Creating healthy communities is an ongoing process. As John W. Gardner said, "The forces of disintegration have gained steadily and will prevail unless individuals see themselves as having a positive duty to nurture their community and continuously re-weave the social fabric." The concept of practice is essential in two ways. The first means simply to *do* community building in the sense of putting the necessary skills to work. The second means to *do it repetitively* in order to improve our facility with community building as a necessary contemporary art form.

It was out of our commitment to the importance of the arts of community building that we developed the Community Building Institute as part of the Center for the Study of Community (CSC). We founded CSC in 1993 as a small, not-for-profit think tank to foster research, thought and action in support of healthy communities. As one of the CSC programs, we developed the Institute, a nine-month course in which leaders who are willing learners came together to learn and practice community-building skills. We will say more about that experience. Before doing so, we turn to the first classroom for more insights into the concept of community—nature itself.

Activity: More Ways to Achieve Healthy Communities

In your journal, add to our list of ways in which to build and sustain healthy communities.

Create a list of challenges that tend to get in the way of building and sustaining healthy communities.

Write a paragraph about what you personally have found to be a success story—one you were instrumental in achieving, or one you know about and admire but in which you were not directly involved.

If you could pick one word that best encapsulates the seed that led to this success, what would it be? Pick a plant you like and, in honor of the seed, name this story the "(Fill in the name) Effect."

Community in Nature

The driving force in nature, on this sort of planet with this sort of biosphere, is cooperation. In the competition for survival and success in evolution, natural selection tends, in the long run, to pick as real winners the individuals, and then the species, whose genes provide the most inventive and effective ways of getting along.

Lewis Thomas
The Fragile Species

na' ture, noun. the system of all objects and phenomena in space and time.

It can be said that humankind has shared at least two compelling urges, designed by evolution, that formed the basis for all beliefs, rules of conduct, and ways to address survival. The first is framed in how we strive to understand and coexist with the natural world and our role within it. The second is how we get along with each other as humans. Here we will address both of these and explore a way of looking at ourselves, our relationships to one another, and our planetary home that can be used as a foundation for creating healthy communities of all kinds. We look to nature as a guide for principles by which people can more effectively get along with one another in varied communities and rapidly changing times.

Principles of contemporary ecological perspectives can help us detect some of the attributes that are central to the healthy evolution of living systems.

Activity: Nature's Touch to the Heart

Think about your most inspiring personal experience in nature. Sketch it in images or words, or both.

Imagine an exceptionally beautiful place on Earth. Think about its characteristics, and what so draws you to it as a place of beauty. Plan a trip to get there.

Natural Guides to Community Building

I am heartened by the possibility that our social institutions evolve as expressions of deep, natural principles.

Stuart Kauffman
At Home in the Universe

nat' u ral, adjective. of, from, or by, birth; innate; inborn; as, natural instincts.

Most people diminish the influence of nature and exaggerate the influence of culture in shaping our life choices. And yet, nature has been establishing and sustaining successful models of living systems for about 15 billion years. The lessons we can learn from nature are compelling. We apply insights from observing nature to the ways in which we live and work with one another in living communities of many different sizes and kinds.

In this spirit, we offer seven characteristics of natural systems that translate powerfully in designing and sustaining healthy human relationships. We call these characteristics "natural guides to community building."

Diversity

Why would we stay locked in our belief that there is one right way to do something, or one correct interpretation to a situation, when the universe welcomes diversity and seems to thrive on a multiplicity of meanings?

Margaret J. Wheatley
Leadership and the New Science

di verse', adjective. different; unlike; distinct; separate.

di ver' si ty, noun. to make diverse, or various, in form or quality; to give variety to.

The first teacher of the value of diversity is the natural world itself. In ecosystems diversity nurtures survival while specialization favors extinction. A diverse ecosystem has inherent more options for survival than do less complex ecosystems. It is unlikely that any natural disaster can stress a diverse ecosystem to the point of extinction. Diversity assures resilience. Monocultures, however, are vulnerable.

Diversity tends to be an indicator of health in ecosystems. This reminds us to think in terms of the many ways in which people choose to learn and participate in civic and family affairs, business and daily life. Diversity is not solely cultural or ethnic. Much diversity is invisible and takes shape in the form of human values, personality characteristics and preferences for learning styles.

From businesses to individual humans, widely varied human organizations have characteristics of ecosystems. Just as there is an evolutionary advantage to a diverse ecosystem, there is a survival advantage to human organizations that are inherently diverse. For example, in times of downsizing businesses, the business will tend to be more resilient to the extent that its employees are able to use a variety of skills. Whatever the size of an organization, the extent to which there is variety among people's talents and interests will tend to enrich the skill base and the capacity for creative problem solving.

Individual human beings can benefit from a willingness to broaden their personal base of interests and talents. This can even affect a person's physical well-being. For example, people who spend decades in a job, without benefit of continual opportunities to learn, will tend to be more stressed by change than their counterparts with a broader base of experiences. Loss of a job, divorce, death in the family—any of life's difficult surprises—can be magnitudes more difficult for a person without a wide range of skills for coping with such changes.

Human communities have the inherent capacity for diversity. Diversity, however, is not solely cultural or ethnic. In fact, overemphasis on the visible differences associated with cultural and ethnic diversity can often be divisive rather than community-building forces. Recognizing and valuing diversity in human communities includes having a respect for preferences in learning styles and behavioral patterns under stress. When in doubt, opt for diversity. That is, be inclusive and consciously respectful of varying perspectives when attempting to solve difficult problems over time.

Activity: Diversity Assessment

Do a mental inventory of the diversity in your life. Remember that diversity can mean far more than cultural and ethnic differences. Which settings and communities in your life are the most diverse? Which are the least? Think about what you consider to be the strengths and weaknesses of each.

In your journal, make two columns, one titled "most diverse" and the other "least diverse." List those communities under the columns in which they best fit. On the far right of the page, leave room to write about the strengths and weaknesses of each.

Then, in your journal, write a sentence next to each community you listed that states what you personally could do to change those things you don't like, and support those things you do like, about them.

Change

> *America's fate and direction depend on citizen leaders in every nook and cranny of our great nation. Change will come ... not from the top down but from the millions of people like you and me raising our voices from the bottom up.*
>
> Marian Wright Edelman
> Founder, Children's Defense Fund

change, verb. 1. to alter by substituting something else for, or by not giving up for something else. 2. to make different; to convert.

change, noun. 1. a substitution of one thing for another. 2. any variation or alteration.

Nature is constantly in a process of change. In the large view, change tends to be evolutionary. Even dramatic changes take place within a framework of overall dynamic stability and continuity. Our human tendency is to have some fear of change, especially sudden change or changes we cannot control. There are many positive, proactive approaches we can consciously employ to work constructively with this natural process.

In terms of natural and cultural systems, we recognize two major qualities of change: imposed change and emergent change. Because of our gifts of consciousness, humans are facile at imposing change. Imposed change is something we do to something else. Emergent change is change that we experience from causes beyond our control.

Here is an example. Vaccines and immunizations are changes that we impose upon microbes and germs. Germs in turn adapt to the changes we make in them and adjust their life forces to accommodate those changes. We then witness the emergence of new resistance to our imposed changes. Historically, humans have been better at imposing changes that cause things to happen rather than developing the more passive skills of seeking evidence for emergent change. We seem to prefer taking charge and doing something rather than investing in the contemplative and reflective acts that accompany emergent change.

Change is continuous in all systems. Often human urges toward action interfere with our ability to recognize the subtleties of those nonhuman changes that guide the soul of the evolutionary processes. Unless we learn to read emergent changes in the context of natural systems, it is likely that the knowledge we accumulate will be more of an indication of how we cause change than of how we respond to change.

Activity: Personal Capacity for Change

Think about the various settings, such as family, friends, profession, lifestyle, habits, preferences, in which you exercise your capacity for change. In your journal, on a scale of 1 to 10, mark where you think you stand with respect to your capacity for change in each.

Do the same with a few additional settings that you choose on your own.

Create a column for "emergent change" and one for "imposed change." Put examples from your daily life in each column. Indicate, for example, what instances of emergent change you observed today. What, if any, imposed change did you personally take action to effect?

Overall, where do you think you settle with respect to your capacity for change on that scale of 1 to 10? If you think you'd like to adjust the scale, making yourself either more or less prone to select change as a personal option, try it for a week in at least one of the areas that matters most to you. You might try family before you try profession, or vice versa—just to ease into the concept!

Niche

> *You can do public work with people you don't like, you don't agree with, whom you wish you didn't see ... You recognize the need to do public work together. In that process, you do begin to create relationships and you certainly create a culture that is decent, a culture of respect.*
>
> Harry Boyte
> Center for Democracy and Citizenship

niche, noun. a place, condition of life or work.

A niche, in the ecological definition of the word, is how an organism makes a living. Every organism has a niche and is therefore inherently important. When we actively apply this concept to our relationships with one another, it can be palpably felt. Walk into a setting where everyone has a voice and treats everyone respectfully and you quickly notice the peaceful good humor that pervades. Disagreements still occur; however, there are processes for resolving them, and everyone participates. What is most important about the application of this concept is that it be authentic.

The first definition in our dictionary refers to a niche as a "recess in a wall where objects may be placed." This definition mirrors the tendency for over-compartmentalization that exists in traditional science.

Consider the difference between "niche" as a compartment and "niche" as a role. As a compartment, the word rings of the dreaded cubicles of the comic strip Dilbert—a place of isolation and fixed expectation. Used to indicate a role, the word is alive with possibilities—each person can have multiple niches, and various niches over time. A niche requires action. An organism has something to do. Every organism warrants respect.

One of the limiting characteristics of early biological science is the tendency to classify organisms in terms of their complexity. It has seemed perfectly normal for humans to perch on the highest limb of the tree of life, distributing all else below and considering all else to be less important than humans. Hierarchies bring with them the baggage of superiority. That is one of the most powerful messages of contemporary science. It is evident in evolutionary and ecological terms that all organisms, if they are here now, are successful survivors in the evolutionary sweepstakes. They evolved into the forms they now possess. In a sense, each stands on a stage of equivalence—each is a survivor through the patterns of billions of years of life on this planet. Only the success stories are here. Contemporary ecology requires us to recognize this fact.

It is important that we recognize this concept in our human relationships. We cannot treat one another hierarchically and still preserve the freedom and dignity that is inherent in the gift of human life. No less than an overturning of our ill-gotten arrogance can restore us to an honoring of equivalence. We each must learn the skills of respect for life in all its varied forms with all its many roles. Life is the process that binds our mutual future into an expression of a viable shared destiny.

Activity: Niche Detector

Think of examples of circumstances you know of in which people are treated disrespectfully. Identify three things you can do about each of them. Pick one—and do it.

Check your results, and keep at your efforts to minimize the times that people around you are treated with disrespect. Persistence pays, and it benefits the common good.

Competition and Cooperation

> *We are essentially cultural animals with the capacity to form many kinds of social structures, but a deep-seated urge toward cooperation, toward working as a group, provides a basic framework of these structures.*
>
> Richard Leakey and Roger Lewin

com pe ti tion, noun. 1. the act of competing; struggle or rivalry for supremacy, a prize, etc. 2. a contest for some prize or honor, an advantage.

co op er a tion, noun. an act or instance of working together for a common purpose or benefit; joint action.

e co lo gy. mutually beneficial interaction among organisms living in a limited area.

Although competition exists in natural systems, its role has been overemphasized. Cooperation is prevalent and actually more pervasive than the role of competition in the natural world. Plants and animals live in dynamic relationship to one another in diverse kinds of living communities. Healthy communities have historically been characterized by cooperation in numerous forms.

Cooperation cultivates communication and instills connectedness. Cooperation tends to facilitate learning. Cooperation nurtures a sense of shared purpose, efficacy and accomplishment. Mentoring and intergenerational learning are forms of cooperation. Public/private partnerships are as well. In the world of business, for example, there is a constant dynamic tension between finding areas of common concern around which to collaborate in order to serve the interests of consumers and the economy overall, versus maintaining competitive advantage in a business sense.

Civic life in this country is being dramatically affected, for the positive, by a trend in the past 20 years to foster collaborative community problem solving. In recent decades the influence of collaborative and cooperative approaches to learning in schools has grown significantly as well.

Competition is a highly threatening experience for many, particularly if one is not a willing participant who has chosen to play. It appears most often as a form of forcefulness and aggression. We find ourselves caught up in a contest that seems out of our control. One-upmanship, strident questioning, and forcing people to become defensive are common strategies used by people who elect to bully others. If you are not a willing participant in a competitive process, your emotions may quickly jump into the fray. You may feel bewildered and confused.

However, if those involved have willingly entered a competitive setting, the spirit of play dominates and each participant knows the rules and limits of the game.

This can take the form of a quest for personal excellence. Such competition is seldom threatening. It can be invigorating.

Just as there are consequences to competition in human affairs, so too are there in the natural world of ecosystems. People often make forceful arguments about how the natural world is a "dog-eat-dog" environment governed by the laws of tooth and bloody fang. This is good stuff for pulp novels but it is not as accurate as once thought. From an evolutionary perspective, cooperative interaction among species in ecological systems is more prevalent than competition.

Nature has been the quiet bystander to all manner of human interpretations in which it is claimed to be savage and humans are said to be civil. The laws of natural selection have become the shibboleth—the survival of the wisest—for those who choose to create laws of society that are parallel to Charles Darwin's propositions for the evolution of the species.

As the study of nature has increased in the years since Darwin lived, it has become clear that competition is insufficient for explaining either evolution or ecology. Field scientists the world over have begun to recognize that cooperation is a far better process for explaining what is happening in nature, now and in the past. Clearly there are aggressive, territorial and violent behaviors, but, for the most part, these are localized and infrequent. Nature progresses by getting along. In the game of life, nature plays to stay in the game while humans play the game to win. Nature does not give us permission to compete, so we must question the reflex toward competition in human affairs.

Words related to competition include winning, beating, overwhelming, devastating, destroying, striving, struggling, clashing, colliding, conquering, killing and driving them back. Words that connote cooperation include helping, nurturing, assisting, guiding, uniting, partnering, combining, joining, facilitating, harmonizing and sticking together. Learning to see cooperation in nature provides a clearer view for seeing it in human affairs as well. If competition exists in nature, then cooperation does as well. When we balance the tendency to compete with a tendency to cooperate, we will take a giant step toward civility, community health and peace in the world.

Balance the tendency to compete
with the tendency to cooperate
and we will take a giant step
toward peace in the world.

Activity: Tally the Two C's

Make a list in your journal of the ways and settings in which competition serves you in your life. Do the same for cooperation. Be alert to both throughout one full day. Be aware of how you feel in each circumstance. Note whether you tend to be more relaxed, less stressed, in one circumstance or the other—and which you prefer.

Make two columns in your journal. Title the first column "competition" and the second "cooperation." During a 24-hour period, keep track of when you compete and when you cooperate. Note the time, duration of the activity, and a one-sentence description of the circumstance. At the end of the 24 hours, tally the numbers. Which, if either, do you do more than the other? Think about the nature of that 24 hours. Reflect on whether this seemed to be a typical day, and whether it required more than one kind of tendency than the other. Write one page to summarize your thoughts about the ways in which you tended to compete or cooperate, or both.

Mark your calendar for two weeks from now. Do the exercise again. Notice the similarities and differences, and write about the results.

Consider your environment. Pay attention to whether those around you, whatever the setting, appear to be cooperating or competing with you.

Self-Regulation

The frog does not drink up the pond in which he lives.
Traditional Saying

reg u late, verb. 1. to control or direct by a rule, principle, method, etc. 2. to adjust to some standard or requirement. 3. put in good order.

self reg u lat ing, adjective. adjusting, ruling, or governing itself without outside interference.

self reg u la tion, noun. control by oneself or itself.

Self-regulation is one of the most provocative natural guides to community building. Its mystery lies in the notion that when we see someone do something or take some action, we have no idea whether the person is acting in the name of conscious choice, inattention or reflex. If it is reflex, as the purists of behaviorism would argue, then the act is a mechanical response to some previous experience or stimulus. Choice is not involved. If, however, the person under observation makes a choice and decides what action he or she chooses to take, then self-regulation guides the outcome rather than reflex.

Some humans abdicate the responsibility for self-regulation by simply giving the power of choice to others. For example, the concept of governance in different cultures provides a way to look at self-regulation by its absence. In totalitarian regimes, individuals are expected to give the responsibility for governance to those in charge. Self-regulation is relinquished for obedience to external forces. This is manifest among leaders who equate power with control.

Contemporary views of ecology and ecosystems hold that the natural world is a self-regulating system. The central dynamics of natural systems are those that have developed through time and have met with lasting success. As the scholar Erich Jantsch noted in his classic, *The Self-Organizing Universe,* nature is the most successful management system in the world. It has persisted through immense spans of time and is still here and functioning.

Within humans, self-regulation is tied to accountability. Self-regulation is a discipline and a foundation for lifelong health. It is also a habit of mind, spirit, and body.

Communities throughout the United States are taking more local responsibility for the quality of life in their environments, depending less on government and big business and looking right at home and in the neighborhoods for leadership. Ed Keller and Jon Berry report in their book, *The Influentials,* that this shift occurred notably between 1992 and 1995. Their observations are based on close to 40 years of comparative research. We interpret this shift in part as an example of people taking personal responsibility through self-regulation.

Similarly, the burst of efforts to establish democracies and free societies throughout the world is tied to this capacity to self-regulate. One of the most compelling challenges in the world today is that of rebuilding communities in war-ravaged environments. And yet, it is a challenge filled with hope. It is the capacity to self-regulate that is making it possible for new nations to form, with new leadership. It is what allows conflict-ridden communities to restore order—enabled by the individual self-regulating actions of many people. Nothing will maintain peace more effectively than the individual actions of many, combined into a self-regulating whole with a commitment to safety, health and well-being.

When we apply this concept to schools, we instantly see that most young people have the capacity to keep their energies and emotions in check, to discipline themselves, to establish rigor, and to take personal responsibility for their actions. Clear ground rules, established through good communication and shared responsibility, provide a context within which students' capacities to self-regulate can flourish. Self-regulation is analogous to an internal locus of control. Those students who internalize responsibility for outcomes, and see a relationship between effort and accomplishment, tend to achieve in school settings. Success as we define it nurtures the human capacity to self-regulate.

When principles of community building are applied, healthy schools can become learning communities in which everyone takes responsibility and feels accountable for the overall climate in which learning takes place.

When students participate in the process of setting the ground rules for behavior, communicate them to one another, and actually own them personally, effective compliance with those rules is more likely. Discipline problems are virtually nonexistent in school environments where self-regulation dominates in student and teacher behavior.

Applying this concept to family and home helps keep tempers in check. Harsh words that cut to the heart are spoken infrequently and energies stay in balance. Family members are able to focus on what matters, and not what hurts. It starts with self-knowledge and practicing the arts of self discipline, which really is what we are calling self-regulation.

Nothing will maintain peace more effectively

than the individual actions of many,

combined into a self-regulating whole

with a commitment

to safety, health and well-being.

Activity: Personal Guide to Self-Regulation

Think about where in your life you are most successful at exercising self-regulation. List the categories in which you are most successful—such as balancing work and personal activities, keeping healthy and exercising regularly, making time for friends and family, and managing your emotions in times of stress.

Now make a list of those areas in your life in which you are most challenged to exercise self-regulation. It could be the same list—such as balancing work and personal activities, keeping healthy and exercising regularly, making time for friends and family, and managing your emotions in times of stress.

Put a continuum under each list, with "most successful" at the far left and "most challenged" at the far right. For each category, mark a place on the continuum for how you handled it—one week at a time. At the end of each week, review your results.

Look for patterns. Set a goal for yourself in each area, to achieve the kind of balance you personally are seeking. If it is to be most successful in each area, terrific. If it is to keep track of those areas in which you are persistently challenged, that too is useful. Use this tool as a Personal Guide to Self-Regulation.

Optimization

> *Great ideas come into the world as quietly as doves.*
> *Perhaps then, if we listen attentively, we shall hear the faint*
> *flutterings of wings, the gentle stirrings of life and hope ...*
> *awakened, revived, nourished by millions of solitary*
> *individuals whose deeds and works every day negate*
> *frontiers of the crudest implications of history.*
> *Each and every one of us builds for us all.*
>
> Albert Camus

op ti mal, adjective. best, most desirable.

There is an unfortunate tendency in contemporary Western culture to think that most is best. The popular sayings, "He who dies with the most toys wins," and "Everything to the max," reflect this tendency. From a distance, primal people of the planet seem to have lived lives that demonstrate a balance. Yet even gatherers and hunters sometimes dabbled in excess as testified by Stone-Age stampedes of ancient bison, extinction of species by early human predation and loss of regional productivity by overuse.

The resource base for nearly all things in nature is balanced and abundant. When nature overproduces a resource, the resource lies dormant until environmental conditions change significantly and the resource is needed. A good example of this is seen in mangrove swamps.

Mangroves are border plants with their roots embedded in shallow estuaries and their leafy top-sides thrust into the air above the reach of high tide. They are stable under normal conditions and produce heavy crops of leaves that fall into the water and sink to the zone at the depths of the roots, providing sustenance for the plants. Normally, far more leaves join the detritus levels than are needed. Is this wasteful? No. The surplus of leaves is locked into the estuary bottom, and is the precise resource needed when a hurricane or typhoon rips the swamp to shreds. Without the productive leaves at the mangroves' tops, the plants die back. Not for long, however. Seed pods from mangroves many miles away come floating on tides. When they first fall into the sea, the pod floats like a stick upon the water. Gradually, they become waterlogged and one end sinks so that the pod points downward. It becomes heavier and eventually sinks downward in the once-surplus detritus where it stabilizes and takes root. The cycle begins anew.

Nature keeps energy and resources in reserve. Rather than maximizing a particular variable, nature tends to optimize its use of multiple resources. The human idea of saving for a rainy day is a form of keeping energy in reserve. When we pace ourselves and avoid burnout, we are acting optimally. Classic burnout is working to the max. Nature reminds us to be moderate rather than excessive. This does not mean we don't work hard nor that we don't strive for excellence. It does mean that we nourish ourselves and others along the way.

Schools that function optimally tend to be pleasant, calm, happy and not stressed. Administrative offices that work optimally in the face of grant deadlines, board meetings, budgetary challenges, and personnel issues are also characterized by a healthy grace rather than a stressed-out, frayed-at-the-edges mentality. Health, family relationships and personal satisfaction are all associated with optimizing rather than maximizing the moments of our daily lives. Clear deadlines, clear expectations, realistic goals and habits of pacing oneself are all tools to help effectively optimize strengths and interests.

Whereas the health care field has a growing understanding of these concepts, such as in approaches to preventative medicine, the business community is demonstrating an understanding of this concept in spotty and inconsistent ways. Maximizing profits is a short-term lifestyle; optimizing profits with sustainable resources is a long-term strategy for success.

The new communications technologies add to the frenzy. With immediate access to people more easily than ever before, the rates at which decisions are made and actions requested are escalating in frequently inhumane, and certainly less-than-optimal, ways. Beepers, personal digital assistants, mobile phones, fax machines and laptops all play a part. Each of these technologies creates convenience but each also contributes to an environment of such accessibility that people are increasingly frayed and fragmented. Email and phone calls can reach us nearly anywhere, and they do, in enormous volumes. All the more reason to self-regulate and optimize, saving some energy in reserve.

Activity: Optimization Check List

Make your own personal checklist of those areas in which you want to pay special attention to living optimally. As a place to start, look at your Personal Guide to Self Regulation. The topics could be the same. Each week, assess how you are doing in each category. Are you burning out or feeling rested and balanced? If the latter, you are probably living optimally. If not, make a conscious choice to adjust how you are approaching the area, whether it is work, family, recreation or whatever else is of importance. This is an overall lifestyle issue. It can help to assess each of the major parts, and then think about your overall approach to life.

Here is another approach. List each of the following (all cues to living optimally) along the left side of a page in your journal: laughter, peaceful relationships, learning, good works, healthy eating, plenty of rest, exercise, recreation, hobbies, professional accomplishment, personal energy, progress in financial nest egg and personal nourishment. (You may wish to use these as a start, or fill in your own list.) Across the top, enter dates for the next two weeks. Leave a space under each date to check "yes" or "no" in each category to indicate whether or not you think you've optimized in that category. Track the number of "yes" checks you achieve in the two week's time. Start another two weeks. After a few months, see if you think you are moving in the right direction for yourself. If not, get a fresh start and try again.

Connectedness

If there is radiance in the soul,
it will abound in the family.
If there is radiance in the family,
it will be abundant in the community.
If there is radiance in the community,
it will grow in the nation.
If there is radiance in the nation,
the universe will flourish.
Lao Tzu

con nect, verb. to bind or fasten together; join or unite.

A major failing of the Western view of education and wisdom has been that we subscribe to the premise that by dividing, separating or classifying, we become more intelligent. Much of schooling has to do with discrete separation of knowledge—physics, chemistry, history, mathematics, astronomy, medicine, literature, philosophy, etc. Each of these is a manifestation of the single, seamless world of the universe, and yet we seem to feel more empowered if we repackage them into supposedly manageable portions. The illusion created by the separation becomes the overarching premise, and we never get the vision of the world as a unified whole. Our task in contemporary times is to learn how to again read nature as a self-regulating, coherent system. We must learn again to see things whole and connected. We must learn and relearn to read the patterns and to see things in context.

In nature's ecologies, every part is connected to every other. The ripples of any action affect whole living communities, sometimes in ways not seen.

Echoing others before him, the naturalist John Muir observed, One touch of nature makes the whole world kin. When we internalize the concept, as we can observe it in nature, that all things are connected, it helps us to remember that such connections are healthy and to be nourished.

In school communities, this reminds us to create opportunities for all students, of all ages, to feel a sense of shared purpose with one another, to be mutually supportive of one another. Everyone in a school community has a commitment to the process of learning. It helps when whole school communities work together on a mission and goals, when there is agreement and shared commitment to instructional objectives and learner outcomes.

Communications devices such as online communities of interest and chat rooms, newsletters, television broadcasts, and other approaches to cultivating a sense of shared belonging through access to information are generally helpful.

New technologies can be powerful allies in this regard. However, these electronic media cannot replace the need for physical person-to-person contact. John Naisbitt's "high tech, high touch" concept still prevails. We need both. Humans need to balance the experiences moderated through electronic and other high-tech devices by also maintaining intimate contact with other humans and the natural, living world.

To serve some of the physical needs, we also need gathering places. The Starbucks coffee folks figured this out-the need for safe gathering places for what the futurist Faith Popcorn has called a "small indulgence"—in this case, high-quality coffee at a slightly extravagant price. The approach speaks to people's yearning to connect with others, even if, as Starbucks CEO Howard Schultz once observed, the customers often don't engage in conversation with one another.

Bring people together in various forms of celebration and activity. Work together to accomplish tangible results. There are many approaches to cultivating a healthy community in which people of all ages recognize that they are genuinely connected to each other.

It is a whole world that we live upon and within. Whether we are focusing on nature or the world of human affairs, a reflex toward connectedness serves us well. Connectedness supports sympathy and empathy. The act of connecting may well determine the quality of the future we share in all communities on Earth.

Bring people together in celebration and activity.
Work together to accomplish tangible results.
The act of connecting may determine
the quality of the future we share
in all communities on Earth.

Activity: Connecting with the Connections

Think of five ways in which to increase the sense of connectedness you experience in your daily life. Do each.

Connectedness is fundamental to community. List three ways that connectedness is functioning well in a community in which you are a member. List three ways in which connectedness is dysfunctional. Work with each, working to sustain the ways in which connectedness is thriving, and working to decrease the dysfunction within those that are not.

Activity: Natural Guides to Community Building

With all seven of the Natural Guides to Community Building in mind as background, go outside into nature and find an example of one or more of the Natural Guides. Without doing harm to the environment, bring back evidence of some kind to demonstrate that you have found an example.

Record your observations in your journal.

Reflect on how these Natural Guides seem to fit, or not, in the context of the many community-building settings in which you live and work.

Communities of Place

If the word community is to mean or amount to anything, it must refer to a place and its people ...
An authentic community is made less in reference to who we are than to where we are.

Wendell Berry
The Art of the Common Place

We have had lively arguments with a number of our friends who share our concerns about the health of communities. Carl Moore, professor emeritus at Kent State University and a vital facilitator of community-based work, comes instantly to mind. Carl believes that "community is in the struggle." While it can come as a result of struggle, we think that definition is too limited. Similarly, Carl is concerned about definitions of community that venture beyond "place." We are not.

While we believe in the importance of physical, geographically bound communities of place, we consider them to be only one form of community, granted an important one. For many people in the world today, however, communities of place are not communities of peace. Take as examples those many areas in the world where warfare dominates. Those physical communities are not peaceful communities, although there are often people within them doing everything possible to bring peaceful resolution to the conflicts that are found there.

People can be grounded in peaceful, nourishing communities of place in local environs and also participate in communities of shared interest, consciousness, and conviction that span the planet. In places of conflict, it is the communities of interest that provide some of the richest sources of hope, enabled by the extraordinary communications capacities of these times, whether by television broadcast, use of wireless phones or access to the Internet.

For many people in the world today,

communities of place

are not communities of peace.

We believe that people today exist in, live in, and experience a wide variety of different kinds of communities. We think it is optimal if people are connected to and live within a healthy community of place where the home is safe, the civic culture is engaged and responsible, the physical environment is free of pollutants, the aesthetics are pleasing, children can walk, run, learn and play in safety, and a sense of encompassing well-being pervades. All of this is good and nourishing and tends to be associated with the mental and physical well-being of its individual members.

That is one goal to strive for. Beyond that, we each participate, or most do, in a variety of communities of social construction involving a family, circle of friends, school community, community of faith, business or work community. There are differences of scope and scale as well. Some are simply local, others might span the nation or the world. There are communities of interest, communities of choice, and, yes, communities of place. Some today are bound by no geography at all, and some, thankfully, are still rooted to the ground.

Farmers' markets are one of our favorite indicators of healthy communities of place. Dan Kemmis, former Mayor of Missoula, Montana, and one of the most thoughtful advocates for a renewed civic process, opens his book, *The Good City, The Good Life,* in Missoula's farmers' market. Deborah Madison, innovative chef and spokesperson for the "slow food" movement, which also speaks for growing and cooking food locally and seasonally, celebrates the value and virtues of farmers' markets in *Local Flavors*. We do as well. They serve as gathering places, an important requirement for healthy communities. They offer healthy food, grown locally and typically organically. They nourish much of what is best about "communities of place."

Faith Popcorn identified "cocooning" as a trend in current times, particularly in the United States. The concept is that we stay enclosed in a safe and nourishing place. It is a sign of distance from engaging in the physical community of place. The abundance of wealth, high-tech toys and amenities, and the importance of one's physical home as a place of safety, entertainment, convenience and relative self-sufficiency all combine to isolate us from our nearby neighbors. Most Americans don't need to interact with others in order to meet our daily needs. We have almost everything we need at home as long as the pantry is full and the electronics are working, whether kitchen appliances or telecommunications devices. We no longer grow or hunt for most of our food. We buy a home, and don't build it ourselves. We have entertainment centers and home offices.

The list goes on and on. This is both a concern and an opportunity. The good news is that, while we enjoy these many comforts and there is a place for the cocooning phenomenon, we are also seeing a trend toward reengagement in civic life at a neighborhood and community level.

A priority in this decade is to establish a healthy balance between autonomy and affiliation. Our personal health and well-being, that of our families, and that of the communities of place and purpose in which we participate will all benefit from our active efforts to establish and maintain a healthy balance.

Activity: Cocooning and Connecting, Achieving a Personal Balance

Close your eyes. Visualize your communities of place. Take yourself through the neighborhoods, at home, at work, where you shop, where you worship, or any other physical places in which you spend time. Check out your feelings as you look closely at each. Do you experience a sense of peace? Do you feel at home? Are you engaged actively? Do you feel connected? Write a few paragraphs about your observations and feelings.

Think about the concepts of cocooning and connecting. Do you think you are maintaining the right balance of each in your life? If yes, make a list of the indicators of that balance-and a few notes about how you achieve the balance. If not, make a list of what's not working and write yourself a short list of "to-dos" to improve the balance. Check back in one month and give yourself a report card on your results.

Communities of Practice and Practicing Community

> *While process is clearly important to the overall coherence of an organization, in the end it is the practice of the people who work in the organization that brings process to life, and indeed, life to process ... By practice ... we mean the activity involved in getting work done.*
>
> John Seely Brown and Paul Duguid
> *The Social Life of Information*

Communities of practice. Practicing community. Different concepts, both are important. Brown and Duguid make important contributions to our understanding of communities of practice. Drawing on the work of the anthropologist Julian Orr, Brown and Duguid describe elements of learning that take a form of community building that has real meaning and is relevant in its context. The context they use for illustration is work-related. The elements are generalizable to some degree.

Think of the core terms—community of practice. In this case, the community is a work environment, where a variety of people with varying responsibilities have real work to do. The formal structures are useful but not sufficient. What emerges is an informal communications process that involves more than asking questions and getting answers. People improvise, innovate, and practice; they share experience and information; they tell stories about their experiences and repeat those stories. The result—a combination of elements based in a context where there is a shared purpose to get the work done—results in collaboration to solve problems, cooperation to share information, and a supportive environment in which to learn from what works and what fails. It is all relevant, informing, and useful. These are the basics of a community of practice as we see it (and we encourage you to visit their writings on this subject)—shared purpose, formal and informal communications, conversation to share information and experience with practical purpose, and the real-world context in which to apply what's learned and continually refine those learnings.

Equally important to us is a concept that could be, and typically is, embedded within communities of practice. The concept is "practicing community." For us that means it is important for each of us to have the opportunity to practice skills of many kinds—whether it is a role in which we are not fully comfortable, a technique we'd like to learn, or something we are skeptical about but are willing to try. The reasons are many, the opportunities are important. One of the most important contexts within which to practice skills today is that of community. It involves practicing ways of being that nourish us as individuals, since healthy individuals are an important foundation for healthy communities, and practicing ways of working with disparate members of communities—that is, practicing the arts of community building. One of the principal reasons we developed the Community Building Institute in the 1990s was to create a setting in which leaders who are willing learners could practice the arts of community building.

We have believed for many years in the power of practice. Some of the significance is related to civic work. Practice begins with each of us as individuals, however. For example, there are many ways of being in relationship to one another that feel strange, invite anxiety, kindle the old fears of insecurity, and lead, as a result, to aggressive, defensive, and angry behaviors. One of the best antidotes to such reflexive patterns of behavior is to create opportunities for self-reflective practice. Throughout this book, we make suggestions for how to include such moments as a part of the fabric of daily life. Just as each of us as individuals can hone our skills of peaceful living, we can apply those tendencies to our interactions with others. We can create communities of practice and ways of practicing community where, without manipulation, the tendencies to cooperate and respect one another are celebrated and nourished. Jewel Cabeza de Vaca, a participant in the Community Building Institute, tells such a story:

> *There is something about people coming together and sharing from the heart, speaking their truth and speaking their journeys and the search that we are all undertaking in our lives. That seeking and looking for meaning and fulfillment and how we can share is very symbolic . . . I remember when I was a little girl . . . We had a family tradition of sharing and communicating the joys of the day and the worries of tomorrow. It was a beautiful time. My grandfather and my grandmother were present. They were our elders and our leaders. They still walk with me and live with me on a daily basis and are here with me now. I honor them and acknowledge all the living teachings that they have given me that are conditions for my life.*

Last night [at a session of the Community Building Institute] I was hearing and seeing in your faces the reflections of all my aunts and uncles and cousins when we were five and six. The neighbors would come and join us. We would sit and talk. In the storytelling, the love, warmth, compassion and caring would be there. They would say, you know, Saturday we are going to go and help build Jose's house. Everyone in the neighborhood would pitch in and make the adobes. They worked three or four weekends or a month or whatever it took until the house was erected and the family moved in. It was a kind of community. I never knew at the time what richness and what depth and what meaning they were instilling in me and giving me. I am so grateful for that. I grew up knowing who I was, what I am, how much I was loved, who my community was, who my family was, who my neighbors were. I grew up knowing what the needs were, how I could help, even as a little girl. As a five-year-old, there was a place for me and it was important. We were important to that circle, to that community. Spirituality was important, family was important, community was important . . . To me, that is what I saw and sensed last night . . . Community comes from that depth inside of us to live community every day in our lives . . . The community really is us.

Jewel Cabeza de Vaca
Community Building Institute
Santa Fe, New Mexico

The kind of experience that Jewel had as a child, and so eloquently expressed, is one that had many characteristics of what people look for—and many yearn for—today. Geographical communities of place with family and friends have historically been what people think of as community. Yet, today, there are also communities of interest (with members sometimes scattered around the world), communities of practice (as in the workplace) and communities of purpose (perhaps short-term, where people come together for a finite period to accomplish something tangible). Sometimes people experience a *sense* of community with people far away, and don't feel connected to the people who live near them in their neighborhoods.

In the ideal, our challenge today is to work to have healthy communities of many different kinds. Some will be communities of place, others will be communities of experience, values and ideas. To be sustained, and sustaining, all must be communities of practice and environments in which we have the opportunity to practice community. We need to practice the arts of community building and experience the fruits of communities of practice. Practice is an art in itself.

Through all of this, we can look for and apply the characteristics of generally healthy communities to many different settings. One of the gifts we can give ourselves is to recognize, in these times, that most of us live in many different kinds of communities simultaneously. In some of them, we do experience more a sense of community than a whole community. Part of our work together is to sort out those characteristics.

Whatever the community, its health is enabled by its members having a set of skills—an ecology of skills—to put to work to help further the community's interests and address its needs constructively, respectfully, and collaboratively.

Activity: Practicing Community

List the communities to which you belong. Put a plus sign by those with which you feel the most powerful sense of belonging. Put a "G" by those that are communities of place, involving a geographic connection such as a neighborhood or municipality. Put a "P" by those which are physical, such as your place of work, school, and worship. Put a "V" (for "virtual") by those not bounded by geography or physical space, but which are important communities in which you participate. Do you feel at home in each of these communities? Are you engaged actively? Do you feel connected? Write a few paragraphs about your observations and feelings.

Think further about your communities. Which of those provides an opportunity for you to experience a "community of practice?" Which of those, and some may be the same, provides a context in which you can practice your own arts of community building? Pick one in which you'd like to participate more—whether as a community of practice or to practice community. Do it.

The Power of Story

> *Traditional Indigenous people have always expressed their symbolic culture through the continuous retelling of the myth-dreams that concern their deepest connections within nature. Totemism carries a message about a human society interacting with nonhuman life in a neighborly world. In this sense, community itself becomes a story, a collection of individual stories that unfold through the lives of the people of that community. This large community of story becomes an animate entity vitalized through the special attention given it by its tellers and those who listen. And when a story's message is fully received, it induces a powerful understanding that becomes a real teaching.*
>
> Gregory Cajete
>
> *Native Science: Natural Laws of Interdependence*

The Native American people of the American Southwest have retained a strong tradition of storytelling. Stories are a way to cohere values. They also communicate values and beliefs. Stories are powerful, nourishing, engaging and participatory. Stories help to reinforce the values and ways of being that can, in turn, be practiced over time.

One of the dilemmas of contemporary life in the United States is that our communications technologies, like television and film, have become the new storytellers. They are not participatory; they are vicarious and remote. Valuable and entertaining though they may be, they shouldn't replace the intimate and powerful process of people coming together to share stories through time. The extent to which we honor and keep the power of stories vital in our lives will be a factor in nourishing our health—personally, in family, in work, in community.

Betty Sue Flowers served as an advisor and member of the faculty of the Community Building Institute. During one visit to Santa Fe, she said, "One reason community breaks down when it gets over a certain number, and why high schools with smaller numbers of students have better community feelings and less gang trouble, is that everyone can know everyone's stories. Probably the limit to community is not Plato's 500, or 200, or 150—but how many stories you can really know."

Betty Sue puts the concept of storytelling in the context of what she refers to as transformational leadership. She says, "The transformational leader is a storyteller. Why is this important? It is important because authority can no longer hold culture together. Authority has lost its power. Whether it is in the classroom, with parents and children, authority no longer has the power that it had. So what has to hold a culture together is vision—not authority, but vision—a shared vision."

Following is an adapted version of a presentation that Betty Sue Flowers made to the Community Building Institute.

She describes, in part, her own interest in the power of story and how it led her to work on what has become the most famous storytelling project in recent times, the Scenarios work conducted by Royal Dutch Shell International:

> *I became concerned about the unnecessary suffering we cause by the stories we tell. It seemed to me that stories we were telling about who we are in this culture, and what we might be, were inadequate. If I thought that, instead of just being critical, I thought I ought to do something about it. So I began to speak about this—and I realized very quickly an interesting thing.*
>
> *That is, none of the stories that I really valued could be told within the cultural story that we tell about who we are. That is because the cultural story that we tell about who we are is an economic myth. It is an economic story. The story of values that I was telling could not be told in this story. I realized that if I were going to tell a story of power, I would have to learn how to tell it within the economic myth and that what I needed was training in economics. But I didn't want to go back and get another PhD.*
>
> *At this point, through a magical series of synchronicities too long to go into here, I was asked to go to Shell International and help them write global scenarios—the future of the world for the next 30 years.*

This was perfect as a way for me to learn, because it involved being with a group of 20 economists from all over the world. I could live with them for four months, in a very intense environment, learning how global economists think—and, at the same time, write fictions about the future of the world.

Why were they doing this? Shell International, by many measurements, is the largest multinational corporation in the world. The corporation is very decentralized; that is why they have lasted over 100 years. How do they hold their culture together? They discovered early on that they have to make decisions about the future. What can you know about the future? Nothing except that it is not going to be like the present. That is all you can really know about the future. Yet you have to plan. Most of what we do about the future is to extrapolate the past into the future. What we are doing is just filing the past into the future and calling it the future. That is worse than nothing. That misleads us into thinking we know what the future is going to be.

Shell International wanted a way to think flexibly about the future, but not under the illusion that they knew what the future would be. They devised this method of scenario-building, which is to build two stories about the future that are mutually contradictory. Both are equally plausible, both are highly quantified.

If you heard Scenario A, you would believe it. If you heard Scenario B, you would believe that too. What happens in your mind when you hold two contradictory beliefs? You hold them not as beliefs, but as stories. You hold them flexibly. You hold them as ways to be able to see what is going on, but not as ways to forestall information that does not fit.

It was an interesting process. Shell International tells these stories around the world. They send out, not professional storytellers, but some of the people who have helped to build the stories. After you build these stories, you begin to internalize them. You tell them with a lot of conviction.

The stories are always told in pairs. They tried with three, but people would say, "we'll take the middle one." We want certainty so much, we want security so much, it is hard to hold mutually exclusive ideas. These stories are not like polar opposites; they are just two different worlds of the future. These stories are very powerful ways to hold a culture together. They give people a way to talk about the future without leading them to think they know what the future is.

In 1992, we sent a team to South Africa to write scenarios for South Africa. This was before the breakup of apartheid. We gathered people together from all the movements and political perspectives.

They came up with four very interesting scenarios, all with bird names ... Nelson Mandela himself talked about the importance of these scenarios and the process around them. They were important because people could talk in general terms about a vision of the future without having to fight over the details.

I often think about how I wish that our health care debate—when there was a window of opportunity to change health care in this country—had taken the form of scenarios so that we could talk together as citizens without getting bogged down in details. You couldn't even have a discussion at the time without getting bogged down. How much better to have a metaphor that would encapsulate the vision of the whole and then work out the details later.

I learned something about the power of metaphor and the power of storytelling from these experiences ... The transformational leadership in the future depends on the stories we build.

Stories. Scenarios are a form of the traditional art of storytelling that has been brought to life in a new context today. Use of scenarios has become a powerful, even trendy, part of contemporary business. One reason is that it touches the sacred truths. It is an adaptation of an historic form of communication—one that people today can resonate with, even without fully understanding its power.

Keith Wheeler and Jack Byrne are educators who see the value of scenario-building as a tool for inspiring young people to bring to life a peaceful, just and sustainable future. Keith is the executive director, and Jack the projects director, at the Center for a Sustainable Future in Shelburne, Vermont.

The Center, in cooperation with the Foundation for Our Future and Shelburne Farms, has initiated a new program called "Shaping Our Future." Among the principles and beliefs that guide this program are:

> *Leaders of the future need to develop new vision, perspectives, strategies and stories based on their understanding of patterns in their world.*

> *Young people need positive visions of the future to provide a hopeful context and perspective from which they can assess the violence, despair, cynicism, powerlessness and self-absorption often supplied by the news, music, movies, and other cultural sources.*

The program develops leadership, improves communication skills, and uses the scenarios approach to provide young people with life skills that will enable them to envision and achieve a promising, healthy future.

It is no surprise that all the approaches today to building healthy communities—in families, businesses and municipalities, as examples—include the creation and communication of story. Use of scenarios is only one such approach.

Both the arts of conversation and the more structured process of formal dialogue are important companions to the arts of storytelling for community building.

Peter Senge has helped to popularize the art of dialogue as a community-building tool. Peter takes a disciplined approach to its practice. Whether you do or not, dialogue can be seen as a close cousin to the arts of conversation. No matter what, conversational arts are fundamental to effective community building in any setting. Conversation requires shared responsibility, speaking and listening, respect and adding to one another's thoughts. Conversation is, in fact, a collaborative process. Conversation is a time to practice the art—while also learning more of one another's story and perspective. Conversation also provides a powerful context for learning—acquiring information, practicing disagreement with respect and building intangible bonds.

John Seely Brown and Paul Duguid offer specific insights into the power of story as a way to cohere a community of practice. They do this in part through observations of many settings, including business environments. They note that "constant storytelling—about problems and solutions, about disasters and triumphs, over breakfast, lunch and coffee—serves a number of overlapping purposes." They call this practice "indispensable" and refer to its powers to make things understandable, to inform, to facilitate collaborative problem solving, to cohere information and to share "collective, collaborative wisdom."

In the *Social Life of Information*, they write:

> *Stories ... can be a means to discover something completely new about the world. The value of stories, however, lies not just in their telling, but in their retelling ... Stories are thus central to learning and education ... Stories, moreover, convey not only specific information but also general principles.*

Tyler Norris is one of the most experienced and thoughtful leaders of the current community-building movement in North America. Among Tyler's many contributions, he served as founding director of the National Civic League's Healthy Communities initiative in the 1990s. Tyler says that communities need a story of their future. It needs to be a shared story, built from shared values and understandings.

Activity: Personal Story

In your journal, write two very different stories for yourself—each portraying a plausible, interesting vision of the form of your life in the next 10 to 20 years. Name each story. Write at least a page for each.

We are all here to learn. Write a few paragraphs about what you have learned along your life's journey.

Think of other stories. In each case, give it a name and write a few paragraphs. Think of the story you most want to be in your life. Check back in a few months to see how the story is holding for you—is it who you most want to be? If not, what changes do you need to make in order to bring the story to life in your life.

The New Civic Imperative

Prior to participation in the Community Building Institute, I felt adept at many organizational development techniques and management skills. But I think I gained a lot of insight into the more subtle aspects of empathy, humor and grace at the Institute. A lot of folks seem uncomfortable when dealing with matters that touch on spirituality, for example. At the Institute, though, such discussions had a practicality in the context of community which, after all, refers to those living in communion.

Perry G. Horse, Ph.D.
Former President,
Institute of American Indian Arts

Since participating in the Community Building Institute, I have led countless business meetings. I've tried to make sure all opinions are heard and noted, and I have had amazing success with what once would have been "difficult" attendees. My main premise is that all people have dignity, and they should be able to retain that dignity even if they are "difficult." In the past, I have been defensive and have pointed out each and every way that they were wrong.

Marci Riskin
Architect

What did I learn from being a participant in the Community Building Institute? That we cannot "build" community—the sense of belonging—"unless we care and share." I have come to the conclusion (whether rightly or wrongly I do not know) that it has a lot to do with our sense of identity and self—our sense of bondedness which in itself is the result of the differentiation that we need to have to be biological human beings.

We are acculturated to be tribal members! Yet, unless we transcend that membership, which has a lot of privileges, a "community" will not evolve from our interactions. The opportunity to transcend comes only when we recognize that our "roots" are not our "identity." That recognition, that enlightenment, comes only out of the crisis of understanding. If, during a crisis, we have the courage to walk out into the unsheltered open landscape, rather than crawl back into the cave of our tribal identity, then our interactions will evolve into a sense of belonging with others in the same open space.

Courage is what is needed most. Courage to undertake the journey and the willingness to go wherever the Spirit may take you. If we can accept the call to be a mahatma then "community" will arise in our midst without our even knowing how it came into existence.

Abe Kurien, MD

The Community Building Institute, with a theme of "leadership for the common good," had a goal to develop and enhance the leadership skills of individuals to effectively address community needs. We established the Institute because we saw a void to be filled by people with skills to address complex community problems. We observed this void at a time when we also saw a yearning for and a rekindling of commitment to reinvigorating the health of communities. More than health, in fact, we saw a yearning to connect—to feel a part of community, to feel "at home." Interestingly, since that time, other research has corroborated what we saw. RoperASW's longitudinal research on those they now call *The Influentials* is an example. Over more than 30 years spent studying the attributes of those who tend to influence change and anticipate trends in American society, one phenomenon emerged in the period between 1992 and 1995. According to Ed Keller and Jon Berry, principals with RoperASW, in their book, *The Influentials*, it was during that period that a major shift occurred in which "people started turning inward and looking more to themselves and their personal networks for solutions to their problems."

Keller and Berry elaborate on recent related changes:

> *Increasingly, we see Americans talking more about community affairs as well, from schools, development, traffic, and other close-to-home issues, to far-reaching issues, such as the quality of life in the community and the legacy they are creating for the next generation ... This rising tide of conversation ... is creating a major ripple effect in business, government and other entities.*

We created the Center for the Study of Community in 1993. We established the Community Building Institute in 1994 and conducted the Institute for three consecutive years. Since that time, we have closed both the Center and the Institute, choosing to let the work continue in ways beyond the structure of the specific nonprofit organization we founded and its associated programs.

When we saw the need in the early 1990s, one of the first things we did was convene what we called "A Gathering of Scholars." In the group were the historian Daniel Boorstin, the poet and futurist Betty Sue Flowers, the philosopher Steven Rockefeller, the activist Ernie Cortes, the priest and social commentator Mathew Fox, the businessperson and civic leader Bernard Kinsey, the civic leader and author Mary Beth Rogers, the philanthropist and civic visionary Angela Glover Blackwell, and the social entrepreneur and tribal leader Rodger Boyd. The list was robust, the conversations compelling. All in all, about 20 of us spent three days in vigorous conversation about the attributes of healthy communities, the challenges that face us, and the agenda that needs to be addressed. Out of those discussions we focused on issues of the future—beginning with children and the health of communities for the long term.

One of the gaps that we addressed in those discussions, and in more that followed, was the need for a renewed civic literacy. We saw the need to develop opportunities for leaders who are willing learners to hone and expand their repertoire of skills in order to deepen and broaden the assets that any community can use to help solve tough problems with respect and skillful collaboration.

We began the Community Building Institute with this notion that each of us as individuals has a difference to make, and at the same time, there is a need to work together for the common good. The common good is what is good for most of us, most of the time. There are hard questions embedded in this—about what is good for most of us and in balance with individual rights.

Among the most thoughtful writers and practitioners of the arts of community building today is Dan Kemmis, former Mayor of Missoula, Montana, and now Director of the Center for the Rocky Mountain West at the University of Montana in Missoula. Dan offered these comments at one of the sessions of the Community Building Institute:

> *It occurs to me that this activity that you have been involved with—while it is absolutely unique in the sense that every individual is absolutely unique—is part of something larger happening in the world right now. We are trying to understand what that is, partly in order to help shape the way we go at the work. I am convinced that the way we carry ourselves in the work has as much to do with how well we do it as how deeply we've thought.*
>
> *Let me start by weaving some thoughts about the historical perspective.*

Stepping back about the space of a generation, about 30 years, we notice the emergence of a few movements that I believe serve as the pillars for the movement we are part of at this time. I believe that what is happening here is part of a movement. You can call it a community-building movement—that is as good as any way of thinking about it. Behind the community-building movement are a few other movements. One of them is the environmental movement and the other is the women's movement. Those movements were clear and powerful; they were not anything that could be organized from the top. They were absolutely organic in the way that they arose. Of course, there were leading thinkers that helped to congeal them—but that thought by itself could never have made it happen if the conditions had not been there in the structure of things for those movements to emerge. They have worked themselves to a point of maturity.

My belief is that out of them, and out of a number of other things, there has now emerged this community-building movement that hasn't generally been recognized as a movement. It is not recognized in the press or media as a movement, like the environmental and women's movements were—but my observations leave me with no doubt at all that is what is going on here. The manifestations are so strong and so insistent in so many different places that we have to see that is what is occurring.

Habits of the Heart, *by Robert Bellah and others, was written at the time of the 150th anniversary of the publication of* Democracy in America *by Alexis de Tocqueville. Tocqueville had come from France and traveled throughout the United States as it then existed to try to understand the nature and character of the democracy being practiced. What Tocqueville found was a complex picture, a lot of which was troubling to him. One element of it that was so troubling he had to make up a word for it was what he finally came to call "individualism." He had never seen anything like it before. No one really had. That word actually did not exist until Tocqueville invented it. He had to have some way of describing what he saw as this tremendous kind of self-centeredness in Americans. He was familiar with societies in which people shape and define themselves in terms of what is around them. Americans were somehow much different.*

So, he defined this idea of individualism. He was fascinated by it, but also terribly worried by it, because in the long run he couldn't see how a democracy could function with people going their own ways, pursuing their own aims and ends. The other thing that Tocqueville saw, which became the basis for Bellah's book, was what he identified as "habits of the heart." Tocqueville said that, in spite of their individualism, or somehow surrounding their individualism, Americans were bound together by certain ways of relating to each other.

He said these habits of the heart seem to arise in voluntary associations—especially in churches, but in other places as well, such as volunteer fire departments, quilting bees and barn-raisings. In those settings, Americans, while they are tremendously individualistic elsewhere, have an enormous capacity to come together and accomplish amazing things. Tocqueville saw that these things did not just happen. He saw that Americans were always cultivating certain ways of relating to each other that involved trust, openness, and an ability to hear what everyone brought to the table. Tocqueville was left with this complex, contradictory picture of individualism on the one side, and, on the other side, these habits of the heart.

Bellah and his colleagues decided, 150 years later, to ask about the current state of things. He and his associates conducted in-depth and sensitive interviews around the US and painted a picture of how things looked 150 years later. Essentially what they found was that the picture had gotten more startling in some of the ways that were worrisome to Tocqueville. Individualism had become institutionalized in many ways. Some of the ways in which we pursue individual paths had gotten out of hand—like issues of liability and lawsuits. Politically, we had institutionalized individualism. Bellah and his associates also found that even though they said that most Americans most of the time speak a language of individualism, behind that they found that we continue to speak what they called the language of memory and commitment. So, in smaller circles, we continued to have the capacity to talk to each other in ways that are very different from the way we talk in public hearings, for example.

That is the main theme of Habits of the Heart. *It is a message of concern and at the same time of hope. Somehow, something had stayed alive in the midst of our society that we perhaps would not have expected to remain alive so long.*

Let me give you another example of something we might refer to as a way of understanding our community-building work. In the 1760s and 1770s, in this country, the colonies were governed by a structure which increasingly was understood as no longer serving them. There began to emerge, in every community around the country, small circles of people who were not in the legislatures but who knew things had to change and were willing to take responsibility for beginning to think about what that change would look like. They eventually emerged as what were called "committees of correspondence," where the committee in Boston would be in touch with the committee in Philadelphia and in Charleston and so on. Rather than simply sit back and complain about what was not working, they began to develop a form within the existing form that could eventually take charge of things. You know the rest of that story.

Now I want to suggest an even deeper foundation for what this community-building work is all about. This gets us back to the environmental movement and hopefully to the women's movement. I am convinced that this is not just a social phenomenon, not just a political phenomenon, although it is that too. It goes even deeper. It has something to do with life itself and the evolution of life. There is something driving this that comes out of an understanding that life itself has been threatened. I think that also has to do with the times in which we live. My generation grew up under the shadow of the bomb. This tremendous threat to existence was always in the background. I am convinced that what has gone on since then has to do with the whole issue of life itself. The reason that new forms emerge is because life needs them to emerge. Life is an incredibly insistent phenomenon. It is not about to be denied if it can help it. It will develop what it needs to further itself. It doesn't do that simply in raw terms of generating life, but, for some reason that we can only feel blessed by, it always does it in terms of trying to generate the good life. It tries to generate something that brings satisfaction. It is a mystery too deep for me. What matters, though, is that a deep sense of a threat to life has emerged. It has developed things like the environmental movement. I believe it developed the women's movement. There was a kind of deep understanding that we could not survive without calling on all the wisdom, all the capacity, within the species.

Both of those movements, as they grew and matured, tended to do it in terms that were "over and against." It was a kind of confrontational and polarized way of doing business.

There is no doubt that all of that was required and probably is still required. But I think the sort of wisdom that humans have begun to understand is that such confrontation and polarization can't be the solution. Somehow, in order to serve the deeper purposes of life, we have to be able to come together. That is where I think community building comes into the picture. There is a deep understanding that we have a wisdom here among us that we can only tap into by learning to listen much more deeply, listen much better to each other than we have ever done before.

Just getting thoughtful people together is good work in itself. I appreciate being made a part of that. When we bring good, thoughtful, passionate people together, and create settings within which they can hear each other, something good emerges. I think that is what the community-building movement is finally all about. Whether you continue to meet in anything like this forum of the Community Building Institute, I am convinced that you will go out into different settings and create the same kind of listening, careful, attentive and trusting atmosphere.

Finally, I will say something about the way we carry on the work. There is a tendency built into us to believe that we have to get it all figured out. We think, as human beings, it is our job to think to the solution. It surely is part of our job, we say, since we couldn't have evolved these brains for nothing. However, the idea that we carry the whole burden on our shoulders is a dysfunctional idea. In most settings where I work, and I would guess it is true of yours too, there is a kind of anxiety that we carry into the work. We are always worried about something. We do the work out of a certain amount of anxiety.

I hope to suggest here that, if there really is something much deeper and broader going on, the work is really being done through us. There is a way in which we can trust the work. We don't always have to figure it all out, if we just listen more deeply and pay more attention. If we are more present, we are more likely to get it right than by being anxious. In some way, hope and faith and trust are absolutely fundamental to this. To me, it is probably more important that we think about how to engender and how to spread faith and hope and trust than any of the issues and forums in which we do our work.

There is also the idea of grace. I draw on a classical sense of grace, in which people move out of a whole sense of their own personhood and at the same time a sense of groundedness, of knowing where you are, of knowing the source of your strength. It seems to me that as we do this work, the one thing we might always want to be checking is how gracefully we are doing it. The more graceful we are at doing it, the better we are doing it. In society at large, it seems to me, we need to aim for that. We need to aim for those conditions that allow people to stand in that kind of relation to each other whenever possible.

Another advisor to the Community Building Institute, Milton McClaren, professor emeritus at Simon Fraser University and member of the faculty of Royal Roads University, offered this additional and complementary perspective.

There is a struggle in which we are all engaged, whether we want to be or not. The American historian Daniel Boorstin once wrote of Galileo that he was a man who stood between two worlds—one dead, and the other struggling to be born. I think most of us are living between those two worlds. Although one is not dead, it is rapidly losing moral authority. It still has immense power, immense oppressive power as we see in various ways around the world at times—but it is losing moral authority.

The new, while it is not with us yet, will be. Pieces of it can be seen everywhere around us. The new includes a change in the relationships between the sexes that is more equitable and respectful. There is a new appreciation of the meaning of human diversity in all of its forms. We have tended, in industrial culture, to view diversity as a problem. That is why we like to create lawns. That is why we like to clear the rainforest. These things are messy and seem to us to be untidy. Wouldn't it be nice if everyone wore a size ten shoe? Of course, they won't and they don't. That is not how life is.

As a Canadian, we tend to think of you in the US as our cousins. I would remind you, and I think Tocqueville meant this, that American democracy is the greatest social and cultural experiment in human history. Athenian democracy 2500 years ago, and American cultural democracy as it is expressed in its finest form, represent a great cultural experiment.

It would be extremely unfortunate if that experiment failed. These experiments can fail. These are interesting times for us. We are experiencing the problems of industrial government in Canada. You are too. The current nation-states were created to some extent by the great waves of imperialism of the 17th and 18th centuries. Those industrial nation-states are now likely failing in two directions: One, they are too small and too narrow-minded to work well globally; and two, they are too big to work well locally. They fail in scale on both sides.

The struggle that you are experiencing in your discussions around community is set in the context of the larger world struggle and the larger world discussion. It will not go away. Community is not a cosmetic notion. It is not a real-estate notion. It is a living concept.

I have been struggling with what a community actually does for its inhabitants. I believe that you have to consider the success of a community—and, by the way, the success of an economy—on the basis of at least five criteria.

First, you have to look at wellness. *A successful community nurtures the wellness of its members. This is wellness in the fullest sense of the word, including spiritual as well as physical wellness.*

Second, a successful community has to nurture the participatory capacities of its members. *All of its members must be empowered to participate. Members should not only get to participate by voting, but by shaping the community, by making it their own, by feeling a sense of pride in it.*

Third, an effective community fosters the education of all of its members. *This is education in the most profound sense of the word. It is lifelong learning—but it is not just lifelong learning. You can lifelong learn to be a crook. It is lifelong learning in the service of education. The effective community contributes to the educational development of all of its members throughout their lives.*

Fourth, an effective community nurtures the vocation of its members. *Vocation is an older, different, and richer word than work. It is certainly different than having a job. Vocation is almost a religious term. It is the sense of someone joining the religious community to find a vocation, to exercise a vocation. Vocation is to serve. An effective community nurtures the vocational capacities of the members of the community.*

Fifth, an effective community enhances the recreational capacity of all its members. *The word recreation is not entertainment. The word recreation is exactly what it says—re-creation. It is the creation of new perspectives in life. It is the opening of new doors. It is the experience of different perspectives. It is a profoundly transformative activity.*

These five elements exist in an eco-systematic relationship to each other. Take any one out, and it won't work. This does not mean that you have to emphasize them equally in life all of the time. You do not. There are times when you have to pay attention to some things more than others. In a particular community, in a particular town or setting, it may be more important to work on wellness than it is on recreation at a given point in time. Over the long term, an effective community—and leadership toward the development of such a community—has to address these five elements.

Both Dan and Milton are mentors, teachers and learners. Of the many lessons we can draw from their words, one has to do with mentorship. We believe that everyone has the opportunity to be a community mentor. We would like to spread that idea.

Here is a constructive challenge. We urge everyone, of every age, in every community, to take responsibility for being a mentor to others—on behalf of the good of the places in which we live, and our relationships with one another, including the many kinds of communities we experience and in which we participate. One of our friends, Walter Drew, on hearing that idea, said, "Does that mean we can't learn anymore?" Not a chance.

The heart of being teachers—if that is part of what mentoring means—is that we are learners. We need to be learning throughout our lives. Everyone has the capacity to be a mentor who, in his or her own life, successfully demonstrates a commitment to collaborative community leadership and learning. By doing so we each contribute to what we are calling the New Civic Imperative—which is to be respectfully and actively engaged in the process of contributing to the health of communities, now and in the future.

Activity: More than Bowling Alone

Find out if there is a leadership program in your community or state. If yes, learn who is involved and about the nature of the curriculum. If it looks interesting, explore the possibility of getting involved.

Check out the many forms in which civic life is actively engaged—imperfectly or not—all around you. Attend a school board, city council, planning or other kind of civic meeting. If you already participate in such meetings on a regular basis, participate in a set of different kinds of meetings for a change—perhaps history, arts, environment or music oriented. The point is to stretch yourself, nourish yourself, and think about the attributes in common within each of these community settings. What's working? What's not? Help to invigorate any of the community organizations which you find to be important to the community, and to you personally.

Considering Leadership

> *The final false debate to be avoided is whether what is needed to restore trust and community bonds in America is individual change or institutional change ... The honest answer is "Both."*
>
> Robert Putnam
> *Bowling Alone:*
> *The Collapse and Revival of American Community*

We occasionally disagree with our friend Carl Moore. We don't always differ, however. Carl has done and continues to do important work in support of community building. Some of his focus is on leadership and the arts of facilitation. Here is one example:

> *I think there is a leadership style around commitment to process. The problem is that most leaders are substantive leaders. And, in those cases, they ought not to be the facilitator of a group, but they might be good consumers of the facilitation. They ought to know when they need it. They also ought to know how not to give up their authority as a leader even though they are having a facilitator. You don't have to give up your authority as a leader while having a facilitator. Issues have gotten so complex, one person alone cannot be responsible for the cure.*

You have to enable the group to find answers that serve the group. That takes a facilitative style—especially in the richly diverse groups that you are all committed to working in, or you wouldn't be involved in issues of community. Organizations can get facilitation within themselves by finding people that could be in the neutral role. People like you could facilitate for one another in your vocational or avocational lives, in your volunteer lives. There are any number of ways you can get that capacity without necessarily hiring it. Knowing when you need it and how to get it to be helpful and accountable is part of what leadership is about in the 21st century.

We recognize and appreciate visible leaders. We also value and appreciate that everyone in a community has a leadership role. Each of us will demonstrate that leadership in different ways—some will be visible, some will not. One premise we hold is that leaders who are willing learners already have a demonstrated commitment to using their leadership talents for the good of the community. We respect their talent and commitment. We also believe that they can, as can all of us, learn additional skills and deepen those they have. Complex times require each of us to learn and grow. One of the challenges of our times is for more of us to have and to demonstrate more skills for helping people in community settings of all kinds—families, businesses, municipalities, and more—to work constructively and effectively together to achieve goals of common interest. Determining how we think about leadership is a part of our preparation.

In these times, each of us is a leader. Part of being a leader is to be flexible. There are various roles that we each can contribute. Leaders today need to have the ability to be sufficiently flexible to sometimes stand up, sometimes sit down, sometimes listen and sometimes talk. These attributes are a necessary part of the skills needed for collaboration.

There are varying and sometimes inconsistent points of view about the qualities of leadership that are important, including the role of vision. In one community-building session, we heard, "If you are going to create something new, you really do need an individual vision. It takes someone with some imagination about what could be done. But at different stages in an organization, you don't need that kind of vision . . . My guess is that vision is far more multifaceted than traditionally is written about in leadership literature."

Leaders today need to be sufficiently flexible

to sometimes stand up,

sometimes sit down,

sometimes listen,

and sometimes talk.

Sarah Adeky, of the Navajo Nation, observed:

> *What I have always heard is, "always have the vision," "always know where you are going," "when you are out there, life is not easy." There are a lot of hills and a lot of wooded areas. It is not flat. You have to climb hills and go down too. If you have the tools and the vision, get out and see and there is a way and a path when you get there.*

Another spoke of the role of values:

> *Values are the hardest thing to talk about because we are raised with them. Like a fish in water, we don't understand our values until we are out of the ocean and can understand them from a different perspective. From an intercultural perspective, we say that you don't really understand who you are until you are in a different culture and you are challenged to think about who and what you are.*

Many people gave heavy weight to "willingness to accept responsibility" as an important attribute of leadership. "If you aren't willing to accept responsibility, you aren't going to do anything. The companion item is willingness to take risks."

Carl Moore offered this perspective:

> *If management is about how you do things efficiently, leadership is about how you do the right thing. If it is about that, it has to be about change, or chance, or risk. I don't know how you can talk about leadership unless you can talk about taking chances.*

Risk and imagination work together. If you are the kind of person who is wired in such a way that you are always envisioning a thing that doesn't presently exist, that you think needs to exist or the world would be better if it existed, you can't sit in one place and have that thing come into being. It is all about taking risks, taking the risk of personal failure.

Personally, it makes more sense to me to connect creativity to risk. When you are talking about risk, you are talking about the courage to be creative.

Activity: More About Considering Leadership

Think about what might be universal qualities that could be found in almost any leader. Carl Moore has observed, "One of those is trustworthiness. One of the ways you come to trust another is through consistency—that you can depend on a person doing the same thing next time. The list of universal qualities is not long. One of the things on that list would be spirit. There is a sense of the sacred in the leaders we admire the most."

With these thoughts in mind, consider: What qualities of leadership in yourself do you most value? Do you think of yourself as a leader? What attitudes about leadership do you think are most needed today? Record your thoughts in your journal.

PART THREE

CREATIVITY

Most men and women go through their lives using no more than a fraction—usually a rather small fraction—of the potentialities within them. The reservoir of unused human talent and energy is vast, and learning to tap that reservoir more effectively is one of the exciting tasks ahead for humankind. Among the untapped capabilities are leadership gifts.

John W. Gardner
On Leadership

This is where it begins for individuals. Each of us has enormous creative potential. Each of us can exercise that creativity in ways that nourish ourselves, and the community of the whole, today in the world. We begin by establishing a working definition of creativity—distinguishing between its personal and public forms, using the tool of learning styles as a way to provide practical examples of how to better understand its nature in each of us as well as in groups of people, dimensioning its characteristics in terms of personality preferences (particularly under conditions of stress), and providing some personal guides to releasing creativity through the power of words.

Personal and Public Creativity

We all know of adults who remain intellectually open, who seem to go through their whole lives with a quality of discovery that is sometimes called childlike. This is precisely the correct word for that innocence, playfulness and flexibility to encounter new ideas, putting curiosity before control. This is a quality that lingers in many great artists and scientists into very old age and is, perhaps, the basis for what we call wisdom. We are now at a time when the need for these traits is greater than ever before, for we are constantly confronted with new and different experiences.

Mary Catherine Bateson
Full Circles, Overlapping Lives:
Culture and Generation in Transition

We view creativity as a personal process with public implications. Creativity is the release of talent in tangible and intangible ways that results in a fresh perspective, perhaps original, but always with insight as a product.

We believe that personal creativity is where the process of building healthy communities begins. Each of us, in our own lives, has the capacity to greet each day anew—seeing and breathing its beauty, bringing a healing view to all that we touch.

While some forms of creativity may come out of anger, and may bring attention to pain and the cruelty surrounding that pain, the ultimate goal of creativity is to heal.

We recognize that there are those who would argue that creativity is a destructive force designed to tear down institutions and perceptions in the name of renewal, reform and revolution. We take an evolutionary view. We are cautious about the destructive potential of the creative process—although we do recognize that it can take that form. Maslow, for example, argued that creativity was the destructive tendency that undermines archaic institutions. Rollo May argued that one has to suffer to create. While both can be true, we are sure that there is a profound role for creativity in the healing process.

While personal creativity is where it begins, all creativity has an impact on the whole. Sometimes, through an accumulation of the energies of many creative forces, the result is to bring the awareness to a public state. Sometimes that is known consciously among large numbers of people; sometimes it simply affects the fabric of the whole, in the continuing dance of life that affects all of humanity with the rhythms of change through time.

Jerome Bruner once said that creativity is effective surprise. Personal creativity is a way that we each can surprise ourselves. Public creativity is a way in which we not only surprise ourselves, but a wider audience as well.

The ultimate goal of creativity is to heal.

Personal creativity is a way

we can surprise ourselves.

Public creativity surprises a wider audience.

Because we believe in the power of personal creativity and its capacity to affect the quality of life on every scale, the following section focuses on ways in which individuals can release more of their own creativity. Our goal is to encourage everyone who does so to begin by living a life of greater personal peace and fulfillment, and to bring that fulfillment to bear on the health of communities everywhere.

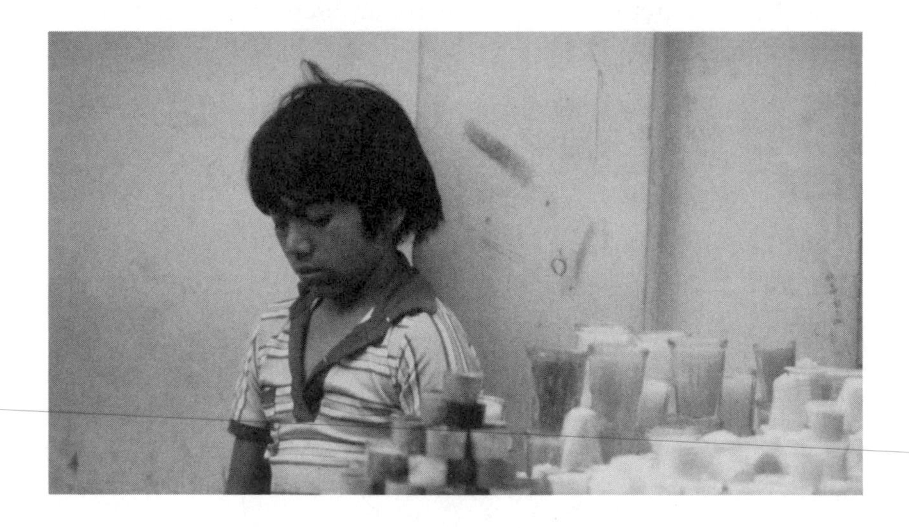

Learning Styles

Great ideas come into the world as quietly as doves. Perhaps then, if we listen attentively, we shall hear the faint flutterings of wings, the gentle stirrings of life and hope. Awakened, revived, nourished by millions of solitary individuals, each and every one builds for us all.

Camus

When we think of community, it is helpful to start with a sincere respect for the differences that characterize the members of any community. While we are more alike than different, as humans, we also have precious differences. These differences need not divide us. They can and do enrich us all.

One of the ways in which differences divide us takes the form of what we refer to as "invisible differences." Those are differences that are not clearly evident. They can't be seen, necessarily. These invisible differences—things we cannot see and may not realize exist—can often be what most gets in the way of our being able to work collaboratively.

We enjoy taking a friendly and easily used approach to learning styles. We have written about learning styles in more depth in other contexts, such as in Bob's book with Bernice McCarthy and Bill Hammond, *4MAT and Science*.

There are a variety of formal approaches that you may take to discerning your own tendencies and preferences. The approach we are working with—based principally on the work of David Kolb and Bernice McCarthy—is simply one of many such tools for exploring learning styles or other such preferences. We take full responsibility for the manner in which we have made the interpretations we will share, and the suggestions we offer for their application to a wide variety of community settings.

Kolb in particular developed a research basis for an inventory people can use to determine their own learning-style preferences. From years of research and successes in applying his findings, he created an instrument called the Learning Styles Inventory that is remarkably effective in determining how different people learn.

McCarthy has focused the majority of her efforts in learning styles research on the application of this body of knowledge to school settings. Her work has produced the 4MAT program, a practical method of applying the use of learning styles to curriculum development and instructional design. We began using the 4MAT system ourselves in the context of schooling. We have now found its applications to work in all settings in which human beings come together to work collaboratively to solve community problems—whether in families, neighborhoods, schools, businesses, church assemblies or entire municipalities.

You may be familiar with personality inventories such as the Myers-Briggs Type Indicator or the Birkman Method. In our experience, these are useful approaches to gaining personal insight, as well as insight into the "invisible differences" that exist within any group.

We believe that invisible differences are to be respected and appreciated. Each of us has preferences for how we like to learn, and how we like to participate in all of life's events—including our work in community. One of the greatest hazards to effective community building is to assume that all of us approach problems in the same way. More common is not even to think about it. Our approach is to recognize that there are authentically different preferences, and that none is more effective or better than another. Each of us can learn from one another, and any group tends to be served well by having a variety of preferences in the mix. That is inevitable in most groups, simply by virtue of the inherent diversity among any group of ten or more people—unless they have been organized by learning style in the first place.

We have taken the work of Kolb and McCarthy and applied metaphoric names for each of the four major learning-style preferences that this particular inventory illustrates. Through more than 25 years of using this model, we have found it to be helpful. It tends to be generally accurate. Here we will provide a brief introduction to our approach. We will follow with some additional detail in a later section.

Here is a simple way to conduct a personal self-assessment of your own preferences. Read each of the following descriptions of an activity and decide which of them sounds like something you would prefer over the others. Think in terms of your first choice, second, third and fourth. After reading all four choices, rank them in order of your preference—from most to least appealing.

Ask a number of community leaders why they take the time to get involved and why they care about the quality of community life. Write or tell a story about why leaders care.

Conduct a fact-based analysis of the number of native and nonnative species of vegetation that exist in your community—or any other fact-based analysis that would be helpful to your community. Document and report the results.

Build a demonstration water purification system to show how a household can conserve and protect water resources—or build something else of practical value that you can do in a hands-on way that will demonstrate something useful.

Invent a way to market and sell tools for community-problem solving—or invent some other way to stretch the edges of people's thinking about how to solve problems within a community that matters to you.

The first activity corresponds to the preferences of the Poet, the second to the Scholar, the third to the Engineer, the fourth to the Entrepreneur. Again, we have applied metaphoric names to each preference—Kolb and McCarthy do not.

After you've picked the activity you would be most likely to choose over the others, see whether the following brief description seems to be a match with your own preferences. Look at each of the other choices you made, in their order of preference. See whether your selections—from most to least preferred—seem to be a match for the kinds of approaches to learning you prefer.

Obviously, these are a short-form introduction to these learning style preferences. Whether your choices seem a fit for you or not, the process is a way to begin to appreciate the notion of invisible differences.

Poet

These are the folks who want to have a reason to be involved. They want to answer the question "Why care?" before they choose to learn about something. They tend to like personal involvement, wanting to know why it matters to them to engage.

Scholar

Scholars like the facts. While the poets tend to have some emotional involvement in what they learn, and how they learn it, scholars don't want to muddy the waters much with emotion. They tend to be good readers, if not listeners, and like going to substantive sources of information. They prefer to approach things rationally, to the extent possible. They are looking for answers to the question, "What?" They want to know the facts.

Engineers

These folks are "hands-on." If something can be built, not just talked about, that is their preference. They prefer to get to action. "How?" is the question they ask themselves and try to answer by doing.

Entrepreneur

These folks like to transform things from what is to what could be. They tend to ask themselves, "What if?" "If we tried it this way, what would happen—or if we took this approach, what results would we get?" They tend to use their intuition, moving quickly to action if something "feels right."

Our work through the years has shown that each of us holds within us the capacity for all of these learning style preferences—and each of us does tend to approach learning with one of these preferences more "front and center" than the others.

Each of us begins the process of developing our learning-style preferences as children. Not surprising, we carry those preferences with us throughout our lives. What is surprising is that we tend to think—even as adults—that everyone else must prefer to learn in the same ways we ourselves do. Even if these differences are brought to our attention in our youth, they are not often acknowledged in the context of families, neighborhoods, work settings and civic organizations, whether city council meetings, public-involvement hearings, civic task forces, school boards or business roundtables. Within businesses and a variety of work environments, we are quick to acknowledge that we have seen increasing attention to use of personality inventories and other devices for discerning different styles among employees. There is still much work to be done within work environments, and even more to be done to carry some of what can be learned from those tools to the diverse kinds of community settings in which we increasingly find ourselves and on which healthy civic life depends.

We offer learning styles as one means by which to understand invisible differences. Our purpose is to increase the options for each of us to stretch our capacity to learn beyond our well-developed preferences and habits. It is also to prepare us for the inevitable variety of people we find in any family, neighborhood, school, business, civic or community setting.

Any learning style is cultivated through habit. Our preferences, however, need not imprison us. Each learning style has value and merit. That we have such preferences need not isolate us but can be a foundation from which to expand our options. In fact, given how the human brain functions, we all have inherent capacities to expand our repertoire of preferences and skills.

If one reason to learn more about learning styles is to expand our individual capacities for effective problem solving, another is to increase the likelihood that varied groups of people will be able to work collaboratively to solve problems—again, whether in families, neighborhoods, schools, businesses, civic, church or other community settings. In fact, by appreciating that there are differences in any group that have to do with how people prefer to solve problems, we can begin to plan for those differences. We can learn to respect the fact that problems will tend to be solved more effectively in a group setting if the group has various skill sets, and therefore diverse strengths.

There is an interesting finding from the world of business that speaks to the power of respecting this variety. It goes like this: Teams of people who have similar learning styles will tend to quickly come up with solutions to problems. Groups of people with a wide variety of learning style preferences tend to take far longer to come up with solutions to problems. Whose solutions endure? Those that come from diverse, rather than like-minded, groups of people have more inherent resilience and tend to last longer when applied in real-world settings.

With this as rationale, in part, for why it is useful and important to learn about how people prefer to learn, here is a framework for understanding these invisible differences in greater detail.

Subjective and Objective

sub jec'tive, adjective. exhibiting or affected by personal bias, emotional background.

ob jec' tive, adjective. exhibiting or characterized by the emphasis upon or tendency to view events, phenomena, ideas, etc., as external and apart from self-consciousness; not subjective, hence detached, impersonal, unprejudiced.

A major component of understanding learning-style preferences is to note the differences between subjective and objective learning. A person who prefers to learn subjectively tends to want the content and processes to be personally meaningful. He or she will judge the worth of what is being learned by asking the question, "What does this have to do with my life? Why is this important?" For example, if such a person is asked to name all of the capital cities of the 50 states there will be less enthusiasm than if the question were, "In which state capital would you most like to live if you could, and why?" The subjectively biased person wishes for personal fulfillment of emotions and feelings as well as knowledge.

People with an objective preference are far more interested in whether what they learn can meet the test of accuracy. They want the knowledge they acquire to be verified by academic rigor. In fact, they prefer that the knowledge they seek is seen as true by the culture at large. An objectively biased person might relish making a list of state capitals or presidents of the United States. Both tasks have a right answer and can be checked in standard references. As youth who prefer objectivity mature, they tend to be drawn to content and methodologies that reflect disciplined scholarship in lay and professional fields. This does not mean they will necessarily be your community's accountants, physicians, or scientists. They might, but they could also be mechanics, pilots, athletes, academics or any number of other things. Each will tend to have a commitment to learning, and testing their learning, against objective measures.

Subjectivity and objectivity are simply preferences. In the long run, one tendency is based on how it feels and the other is based on the data on which it is grounded. People demonstrate their invisible differences when they select, through habit, the means by which they process information and learn. As each of us experiences more success with our preferred style as we live more and more years, we can become less flexible, less aware and less tolerant of others' preferences. On the other hand, if we realize that we personally have all these capacities within ourselves, and that the decisions of any group will tend to be strengthened by the combined use of these different preferences, we can move ourselves tangibly toward greater flexibility and fluency of thinking. We can also be more effective as facilitators of collaborative problem solving in any setting.

Active and Reflective

ac tive, adjective. exhibiting a process in which an effect is achieved or function is performed; the doing of something.

re flec tive, adjective. exhibiting mental consideration, contemplation.

There is another pair of preferences that also forms the foundation for learning styles. People tend to prefer to learn by being active or by being reflective. Many people, for example, feel that time is being wasted if there is not a flurry of activity that accompanies learning. "Don't just stand there, do something!" might be their slogan. Others prefer the tranquility of time to reflect before their learning has meaning. They might prefer a banner that reads, "Don't just do something, stand there!"

Taking action has more popular appeal in a society that emphasizes productivity and results. It indicates that something is getting done. From Sunday school, where we are told that "the devil finds work for idle hands," to schools where children who daydream and gaze out of windows are brought back abruptly to "pay attention," much of the culture puts a prevailing emphasis on the value of action. Moving too quickly to action can mean we did so without enough consideration of the consequences of those actions. On the other hand, too much reflection can mean immobility.

Combining These Preferences Into Characteristic Styles: Getting to Know the People

When we arrange these pairs of preferences into a diagram with two different axes, we can begin to describe the characteristics of people who cluster their preferences for either objectivity or subjectivity, action or reflection, into a combination that can be described as a learning style. Again, these styles are simply preferences. Each of us has the capacity to use all these styles; we simply tend to favor one or two more than the others.

In the diagram below, the subjective/objective preference is plotted on the vertical axis and the active/reflective preference is marked on the horizontal axis. Each of the quadrants represents a learning style.

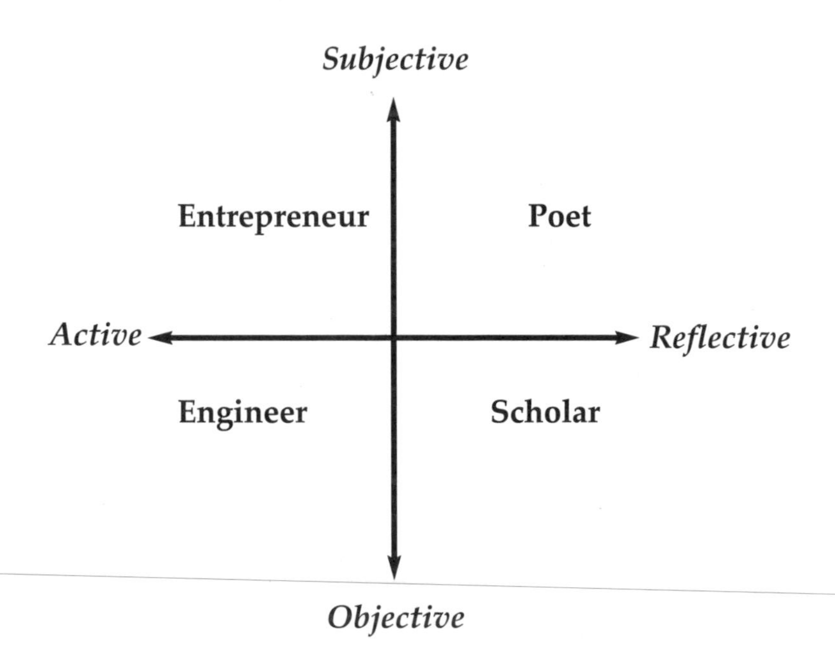

Poet

Subjective learners tend to be deeply immersed in their emotions and feelings. Reflective learners cherish the opportunity to carefully explore the meaning of their learning experiences. We have chosen the metaphor, the Poet, to characterize those people who tend to prefer processing information and experience through a combination of subjectivity and reflection. The Poet likes intimacy and courtesy. He or she tends to value friendship and shows genuine concern for others. Poets find it pleasant to learn by engaging in conversation with others. They enjoy working in small groups where they can get to know others personally. They are interested in the personal well-being of others and often act passionately as peacemakers, resolving problems among coworkers, family members and friends. Poets want what they learn to apply directly to themselves. Remote abstractions are not satisfying. The question asked by the Poet is "Why?" Poets need to know why they should care about being involved in the project at hand. If you can give a Poet a reason to participate, he or she can be a great contributor. If you haven't answered the question, "Why care?," you probably won't get a Poet's attention.

Serving the Poet: Implications for Building Community

Whatever the setting—family, civic group, parent-teacher organization or business as just a few examples—there are likely to be some Poets in the mix. Whatever the agenda, it helps the Poet to have a way to ensure that his or her personal stake will be addressed.

Here are a few examples of ways to plan for the Poet's needs.

Keynote Address

Start a keynote address with a personal story that connects to members of the audience. Describe why you are speaking and why your topic is important to those in the audience before you get too deeply involved in the content.

Civic Meeting

Imagine you and 10 or 15 members of your community are working together to accomplish something tangible to improve the quality of life for children. At the beginning of the meeting, take the time to make sure everyone has the opportunity to say, briefly, why they care about the project—and what they want to accomplish from this particular meeting. Giving each person a brief opportunity to speak personalizes the process, and also cultivates the kind of personal involvement that Poets enjoy.

Business

The manager who walks around and checks personally on his or her employees has the opportunity to hear the Poet's stories and suggestions. Inviting the Poet's opinion and acknowledging his or her ideas with respectful consideration are ways to keep the Poet happy and simultaneously serve the business.

Classroom

Create a feeling of being "at home" in the classroom, or, within a school, having a "home base." Start each activity with an opportunity for each student to speak. That honors the individuals involved, and creates a climate for friendly appreciation of one another essential to the optimal engagement of the Poet. Something as simple as asking "What do you want to learn from this activity?" and recording the responses for all to see is a way to create that climate.

Scholar

The reflective learner likes to mull things over and approaches learning contemplatively. Combine a preference for contemplation with a preference for objectivity and the metaphor of Scholar emerges. In the classic tradition, people with these preferences tend to have an abiding respect for facts. They seek accuracy, order and correctness. Sometimes, in the search for these qualities, these people may not notice deadlines come and go. With a preference for exactness, they often wish for more time to acquire more data, more substance, more knowledge. Objectivity to many means having the "answers" and results that are quantifiable. Scholars ask the question "What?" They want to know the basis for understanding a problem. They are happy to be provided information in a concise, linear fashion. They don't mind listening—in fact, the traditional approach with an expert providing a lecture is quite appealing to the Scholar's tastes.

Serving the Scholar: Implications for Building Community

Once again, if you find yourself in a public setting, you are likely to find some Scholars in the mix. Scholars tend to be relatively patient with the Poet's need for a rationale. And, because they too are reflective, they can wait to take some action. They do, however, need well-organized information that appears to be accurate as a foundation for their interests in being involved in any community initiatives.

Here are a few examples of ways to plan for the Scholar's needs.

Keynote Address

After you've given the Poet a reason to listen to you, and a personal hook of some kind, it is time to address the Scholar's needs. The second part of any keynote address is the section in which you can lay out the facts. Do it concisely, clearly, and substantively—and you will gain the respect of the Scholar. This is a good time to use overhead projections or slides with clear information.

Civic Meeting

Imagine the same group of people working on a civic issue. The Scholars want and need to make sure that the project is standing on solid ground. A briefing based on research, a presentation from experts, a well-prepared overview of the salient facts affecting the situation—these are examples of how to serve the needs of the Scholar as well as the group as a whole.

Business

Invite the Scholar to assemble a team of people to present an analysis of business centers within the corporation. He or she is likely to be good at synthesizing a variety of quantitative data and presenting it succinctly. Use the presentation as part of a strategic visioning session in which the Poets have already established the rationale for the importance of the vision—now the Scholars can provide a factual data base from which to inform the visioning process.

Classroom

Most classrooms in the last several centuries were effectively designed to meet the needs of the Scholar, in the sense that Scholars are patient and appreciative recipients of information through traditional means such as lectures and reading assignments. It is appropriate to serve the Scholar in any setting—with, for example, concise delivery of information in a succinct oral presentation. To only serve the Scholar, however, misses the opportunity to engage the whole brain, and the whole ecology of learners who tend to be in the mix.

Engineer

The unusual combination of objectivity and action becomes clear if we remember times when we followed a recipe to make a meal, or read and used instruction sheets to build a model, or read a manual to install a software program on a computer. Engineers need a conceptual blueprint to provide the basis for taking action. With such a starting place for guidance, Engineers move quickly into action. In no time at all, there is a gourmet meal, a model city and a communications network! The Engineer is a willing partner to the Scholar as he or she quickly finds ways to apply the objective "truths" of reflective colleagues. If the Engineer's urge to take action exceeds his or her concern for objectivity, problems may arise. Engineers tend to fix things that are not broken and live a lifestyle of "Ready, Fire, Aim!" Asking the question "How?," Engineers want to know how to do things, how to put ideas into action. They want to be grounded in solid information. They simply need to work at things in practical, constructive, and, ideally, "hands-on" ways.

Serving the Engineer:
Implications for Building Community

There often are not a large number of Engineers in collaboratively oriented civic settings. They frequently are too busy taking action to have the patience to sit through meetings. However, there are usually a few in the mix—to be cherished for their need to get things done rather than simply talk about it! Here are a few examples of ways to plan for the Engineer's needs.

Keynote Address

After establishing the rationale, and providing the facts, now it is time to address the needs of the Engineer who may be sitting in the audience. Ideally, the Engineer would have the opportunity to take your ideas and try them him or herself. In lieu of that, offer "10 things you can do" or "five easy steps for putting these ideas to work." Put the steps in sequence with visuals. Use a combination of numbered steps and simple instructions interspersed with video clips that show what the process looks like.

Civic Meeting

These folks are the hardest to get in the door to a civic meeting, and the most difficult to keep in their chairs for any period of time. They get frustrated with "process" and have a limited tolerance for seemingly interminable discussions about why something is important. Knowing this, make sure every meeting includes some steps for taking action. Use a timeline with names attached to the goals you set, and a means by which to be accountable for results. Engineers get results. They will put up with the discussion phases of a civic process as long as there is some payoff in visible and tangible results.

Business

Engineers tend to be tenacious. They love to solve problems that involve doing something physical and tangible. In business settings, they'll take a product idea and literally build it. They will invent systems as long as they can follow them through to action. Most businesses need at least a few Engineers to make sure that something tangible gets accomplished. On the other hand, we've seen some businesses, because of their mission, made up almost totally of Engineers. That too can be a limitation if the bias is always toward action without reflection.

Classroom

Engineers are the perfect "hands on" learners. They are the ones who want to actually do the lab experiment, plant the plants, and build the demonstration projects. They are a perfect complement to the other learning styles, those who prefer to observe and make sense of it all, without building it themselves. The shift to more action-oriented, hands-on learning has served the Engineers. Once again, the key is an appropriate, balanced mix of opportunities for each of the learning-style preferences to be engaged and contributing.

The Entrepreneur

Action characterizes the entrepreneurial person just as it does the Engineer. The primary difference is that the Entrepreneur relies heavily on personal knowledge and that perplexing form of making decisions called hunches. This does not mean the decisions are necessarily flawed. Rather, Entrepreneurs often read the edges of situations and see paths to success that few others discover. They are risk takers. People with other learning styles often sense an air of danger in the Entrepreneur. Entrepreneurs learn from everything—they turn all experience into information and knowledge to use when needed. They tend to be casual with the conventions of others. This offends some—particularly the Scholars who are substantively opposite in preference to the entrepreneurs. Scholars are objective and reflective in style, Entrepreneurs are subjective and active. Scholars want far more evidence before they take action than is the characteristic style of the Entrepreneur. Entrepreneurs ask the question "What if?" They love taking an idea and turning it into something else. Invention is their favorite mode. As a result, theirs is often the least predictable of the four learning styles.

Serving the Entrepreneur: Implications for Building Community

Entrepreneurs are in some ways the most quixotic of learners. Because they love to invent and adapt, and because they operate on less data than many others, they move quickly. Most important, if everything is presented to them as complete, they are bored and will look somewhere else to apply their creative problem-solving abilities. Here are a few examples of ways to plan for the Entrepreneur's needs.

Keynote Address

No matter how personally inspiring your presentation, no matter how solid the evidence you offer for your recommendations, no matter how clear your counsel about how to replicate or apply your insights, Entrepreneurs still want the opportunity to turn what you have to say into something that is fresh and unique from their own perspective. So, at the closing of your keynote, put your ideas into a larger context where there is room for the creativity of others.

Civic Meeting

Entrepreneurs are often visionaries. They can take intractable problems and suddenly leap to a creative solution that, when applied, will work in the real world. Their need to get to action can deeply frustrate the Scholars in particular. In the context of a civic meeting or series of meetings to work collaboratively to solve a community problem, make sure there is room for the Entrepreneurs to invent. In combination with the strong rationale of the Poet, the objective substance of the Scholar, and the methodical hands-on accomplishments of the Engineer, the Entrepreneur's insights and tendency to act can be just the right additional element in civic settings. You lose the Entrepreneur's energy and talents if too much lead time is spent on homework that he or she thinks is unnecessary and ponderous, and if you wait too long to test the ideas in the real world.

Business

Many businesses are based on that first entrepreneurial vision that saw a need and moved to fill it. Dreamers who can fulfill the dream through action epitomize the effectiveness of the Entrepreneur. They sometimes can be spread too thin, enticed by the abundance of possibilities for action in the world. In a business context, you will often find one or a small group of these intuitive and action-oriented people. Surround them with the detail orientation of the Engineers and the Scholars and their vision will tend to be realized with follow-through over time. Add the Poets to the mix and the world will hear the story of why the business is valuable and deserves the consumer's or investor's confidence.

Classroom

Entrepreneurs are typically those students who don't fit the mold. They are a burr in the side of many a teacher, walking in the door with all the answers without cracking the page of a single book. They quickly synthesize, and fill in the blanks, without reading everything word for word. They optimize the intuitive leap. Create the space in any classroom for the Entrepreneur to see the reasons of the Poet, benefit from the detail of the Scholar, watch it being built and how it works as the Engineer gets things done. Then leave room for the Entrepreneur to add the unpredictable, the fresh idea, the intuitive leap that makes it all have promise in another setting, another way.

Activity: Valuing Variety

Revisit the four types of learning styles. Now that you have learned more about each of the preferences, have your answers changed? Draw the circle with the four quadrants. Fill each quadrant with just enough color to indicate your own personal preferences. For example, if you are a Poet, fill that quadrant completely. If your second preference is to be an Entrepreneur, fill that quadrant about three-quarters. If next you have attributes of the Scholar, fill that quadrant about half. Finally, if your least-preferred way of learning is like the Engineer's, fill in the quadrant about one-quarter. Take a look and imagine this is your "whole brain." Under different circumstances, you can exercise some capacities more than others. Remember, the preferences are personal. Celebrate the variety within yourself.

Without pigeonholing people, do an environmental scan of the groups of people with whom you participate—whether at work, school, recreation or any other pursuit where you spend a lot of time. Based on these brief descriptions, diagram at least one of the groups using the quadrant circle. Put the initials of each person in the quadrant that you imagine is his or her preferred learning style. Think about the ways in which this diversity of preferences serves the purposes of the group.

Take the four preferences to members of the group. Ask each person to self-identify his or her preferences. You will likely be surprised. If appropriate, revise the chart based on the members' self-identification. Gaining insight is one of the gifts of getting to know more about the learning-style preferences of the people you are close to. The variety is enriching, and those differences are invisible.

If you are in a management role, or even if not, encourage the use of a personal inventory—whether personality, learning, or another kind—as a way for any group of people to get to know more about themselves and one another. Discuss the results. Remember, each preference has validity and diversity, and is an indicator of a healthy ecosystem—whether family, civic, work or in nature.

Intercultural Communications

> *Community is the natural context of human life and activity. We are, one and all, social beings in relation to one another. Our physical and biological survival is intimately interwoven with the communities we create and that create us. The community is a complex of physical, social and psychological relationships that change and evolve through time and the generations of people who identify with it.*
>
> Gregory Cajete
> *Native Science:*
> *Natural Laws of Interdependence*

Just as learning-style preferences are a form of invisible differences, culturally influenced preferences may be invisible as well. These differences can be related to gender, economics, faith and ethnicity. They can arise from generations of influence, and recent life experiences. Just as with preferences related to learning styles, we can never see another's motivation. We experience the result—and we may not even notice or think about the source. Just as with learning styles, it is respectful and helpful to enter any group of people with a view that there are likely to be differences—not seen, but present—that will exist among us. Without preparing oneself and others to greet such differences with appreciation, the group's work together will be hampered. It is the differences we cannot see that tend to get in the way of our effectiveness in working together. Visible differences don't matter. Invisible differences do matter.

Knowing more about invisible differences helps us to understand the varied ways in which people within communities prefer to solve problems.

It is the differences we cannot see
that tend to get in the way
of our effectiveness in working together.

One of the forms of creating, honoring, sustaining and nurturing community over time has to do with a few artful courtesies. One of those is to acknowledge people. Personal acknowledgment is a particularly important courtesy. It conveys respect and cultivates a feeling of being welcome, "at home," and held with regard. In settings where people do not know one another, or are growing to know one another, or even in settings where they do know one another—it is always important to personally greet and acknowledge each person who enters the room. Community meetings are no different than dinners in your home in this regard. Such courtesies can be particularly powerful in settings where people have highly divergent backgrounds and may feel "culturally different" as they enter an unfamiliar setting.

Differences divide us. They also enrich us. One of the first imperatives in diverse community settings is to establish an environment where differences are acknowledged respectfully. Once that has occurred, then it is possible to build a foundation for cohesion and cooperation.

In establishing a safe and respectful environment in which culturally and ethnically diverse people can successfully work together, it is important to acknowledge each person's history. Acknowledgment does not require confrontation, accusation, blame or guilt. It does not require solutions to past problems. It simply allows for what some would call a "level playing field." Feeling welcome is a powerful emotion.

In Santa Fe, more than many communities, there is a strong sense of family and history. That has positives—continuity, rich cultural history, intergenerational traditions and connections. The beauty and the irony is that it is the Native American people and the Hispanics—whose ancestors respectively have lived in the region 10,000 years and 500 years—who hold the power to extend a welcome from a historical perspective. Much of the cultural history of both groups of people is riddled with persecution. One of the contemporary lessons being experienced each day in Santa Fe has to do with the discomfort of the "newcomers" as they feel an unfamiliar discrimination.

Whatever the community, wherever it exists, there will be perceptions that divide and discriminate. We have found it particularly helpful, as a result, to start with the differences that are not obvious. That is why we refer to invisible differences.

We recognize differences that are not tied to skin color or other physical attributes. We start with those differences that have to do with preferences for learning. Doing so quickly moves people's concerns about differences historically associated with "race" or ethnicity—and brings the focus to the enriching common ground of shared learning.

With that as a foundation, it is helpful to move to the broad topic of culture. Respecting differences, acknowledging personal stories, and creating a setting in which mutual appreciation can be cultivated—these are the foundations for intercultural communications and intercultural learning in community settings.

The idea of intercultural communications is to cross the boundaries of cultures. You rarely fully step into another culture; you can come to the boundary, see, and appreciate it. There are ways to facilitate communications in these complex and rich settings. Community organizer Lehua Lopez recommends intentionally including what she refers to as "cultural translators," "cultural facilitators" and "cultural brokers," particularly in any group with deeply different cultural histories. The following definitions are adapted from Lehua's suggestions.

Cultural Translators

These are people who speak the language of the people who will be represented in the group. They are there strictly to translate, in settings where such support is needed. Note that processes will take twice as long, or more, if ongoing translation and use of multiple languages is needed.

Cultural Facilitator

A cultural facilitator is a person who monitors the cultural needs of the different cultures represented in a group. This person may conduct pre-meeting interviews to get a better understanding of the cultures that will be present when the group gathers—including differences in gender and age, as well as religious and ethnic histories. Once in the meeting, the cultural facilitator looks at unspoken communications and body language. There is another facilitator who is actually facilitating the process of the meeting. The cultural facilitator monitors and reports to the meeting facilitator if problems, barriers or frustrations arise.

Cultural Broker

The cultural broker works before and after the meeting. He or she calls the leaders, for example, of the different ethnic groups who will be represented in the group. The cultural broker says, "We are going to have this meeting. So-and-so is going to be the facilitator. How do you feel about him or her? The agenda for the meeting is such and such; how do you feel about that? Is there anything you think should be on the agenda so that it gets spoken about during the meeting?" The cultural broker literally brokers the agenda, the style, the facilitator, so that—before the meeting starts—all the different groups know ahead of time who is going to be doing what and when. If there are disagreements, they get worked out before the meeting begins. After the meeting, the cultural broker again calls the leaders and other key people. He or she may ask, "How did you feel about the meeting?" and "What do you think should happen next?" If there are any disagreements or resentments, these get "brokered" after this meeting and before the next.

Lehua makes this comment about negotiating differences, a process that is continuous in community-building work. She says, "Most of the time, I look for the differences rather than the common ground because it is the differences on which we don't meet and we don't agree and we ultimately fail."

Skills of Intercultural Interaction

Educator and innovator George Otero believes that building one's ability to communicate interculturally begins, in many ways, with perception. He says that, in some ways, any situation is cross-cultural. We agree with that statement.

He also says, "What still fascinates me is that there is as much difference within any cultural group as there is between any of these massive cultures." We agree with that statement as well. Not only is that the case within most cultural groups, scientific research has shown for generations that there are greater biological differences within what are referred to as "racial" groups than there are between racial groups. Once again, we are more alike than different. At the same time, we perceive differences that may not exist—and ignore differences, such as those we refer to as the "invisible differences," as if they did not exist.

One of the skills George encourages people to develop is one he calls "perspective consciousness." He says, "You simply want to be aware of what you are aware of. Then explore multiple views of the task or situation. That will enlarge your options and make for more satisfying choices." According to George, a number of signposts guide us in thinking this way:

You will be less likely to judge or discount your views or those of others outright.

You find yourself saying, "I would never have thought, imagined or believed that," "I wonder," "I'm not sure," "I'm curious."

You really begin to listen to what people who have different views have to say.

You are leery of people who say their view is the only one.

Finally, you find that you are more willing to make a fool of yourself to produce better thinking.

Intercultural communication is another way of demonstrating respect for diversity. It also is a way to foster creativity, innovation and success in collaborative community work. Most importantly, don't take it for granted—and don't take it too seriously.

The first and most basic rules are:
Don't assume you know where another person has walked. Whether his or her life history, ethnic background, family life, or economic circumstance—you can't be sure. The first rule is "don't assume."

Begin by listening—fully, authentically, without preparing your next speech, and without prejudging those who are speaking.

Stay open, even if stressed.

Respect yourself, even if others behave as if they do not respect you.

Respect others, even if you do not agree with them.

Stay committed.

The big challenge is keeping all of us together in a sufficiently coherent whole—that is, in communities—so that generations to come will have the kinds of opportunities for peace and fulfillment we imagine are the rights of all children.

George Otero puts it this way:

> *Start with honor and recognition. People feel safe when they know they are appreciated and respected just for who they are. It is a good idea to recognize all the people and forces that have made us what we are and have brought us together. There are many techniques for establishing such a climate. Do not go forward with your thinking until everyone agrees that community has been created. Remember, community must be created every single time two or more people meet. And, without community, truly new thinking will not occur. Sure, people come up with fantastic ideas individually—yet the world we live in calls for changed thinking in lots of people at the same time. Finally, community happens best when the context for participation is invitational.*

An invitation is an honor, a form of recognition, and a sign of respect.

Activity: Graceful Arts

Think of the settings in which you feel most welcome and at home. Think of those places where you are least at home and feel unwelcome. Identify five things about each that characterize the differences.

Beauty is a powerful friend in creating settings in which people feel welcome and at home. Whether making a meal for yourself to enjoy alone, or gathering friends and family around you to enjoy a meal, pay as much attention to the setting as to the meal itself. A single flower in a vase, the smell of hearty soup or warm bread—each of these can enhance the sense that life is to be cherished. Aesthetics nourish the soul. Make these "graceful arts" a part of at least one meal a day for two weeks. At the end of that time, reflect on what you've learned and how you felt through the process—especially comparing the differences between when you practice those arts, and when you do not.

Learning about tradition and ceremony in varied cultures is another source of insight about the graceful arts. Each month for one year, choose a culture from which to learn. Pick a subject, like seasonal change or child-rearing. Create a collection of stories and examples from each culture. Look for commonalities and differences in the patterns that connect.

Core Personalities

Anyone who tells me that my emotions or desires don't exist is in effect telling me that I don't exist.
Abraham Maslow

stress, noun. physiological. any stimulus, as fear or pain, that disturbs or interferes with the normal physiological equilibrium of an organism. physical, mental or emotional strain or tension.

Community work can be stressful. As we've seen, there will tend to be various preferences for learning as well as cultural preferences. There will also be a range of ways people tend to respond to stress. Having a better understanding of one's own and others' core personalities—specifically, the tendencies that emerge when under stress—can be a powerful part of the process of exercising creativity in the context of building and sustaining healthy communities.

We return to the topic of invisible differences. There are invisible differences among humans that begin with each person's motivation. Motivation determines what drives us, and how we choose to respond to life's influences. Motivation is bonded to our individual beliefs. We can't see another's motivation—and that is why we refer to motivation as an invisible difference. We can, however, see one another's behaviors. The distinction is important.

When I watch another person, I am seeing his or her behavior. I am not seeing the person's motivation. There may be great gaps between what I see people do and what, in their innermost soul, is causing them to take the actions I see.

I must always recognize that any judgment I make is a conclusion from within me rather than from within them. I own the responsibility for interpreting what I see. To recognize and understand the differences between motivation and behavior requires intimacy and empathy. It requires not rushing to judgment.

Our purpose is to provide some insights for each of us as individuals to use in assessing our own motivation—and to caution each of us if we are tempted to interpret what we see in another's behavior. This caution is particularly useful when it comes to observations about stress. One person's stress is another's picnic. What follows is especially intended as a source of insight about one's own stress.

Stress is real and the response to it within a person tends to be visible. What motivates stress is mysterious and invisible. There are patterns associated with people's responses to stress. We organize them by tendencies to internalize responsibility, to be intrinsic, in contrast with tendencies to externalize responsibility, or be extrinsic. We associate these tendencies with personality types—Authoritarian, Dependency Manipulative, and Intrinsic. We named these tendencies in the 1970s, and were substantially influenced by the work of psychologist O.J. Harvey at the University of Colorado.

Stress is a personal thing. For example, one of our friends parachutes from aircraft while another free climbs on extremely hazardous mountain faces. Both find their sports exhilarating. Both are extremely uncomfortable speaking in public. When someone experiences physical, mental or emotional tension, a typical response on the part of the person experiencing the stress is to try to resolve it or "get rid of it." Our responses tend to become habitual, reflexive. Each time we successfully resolve the stress, we are more likely than not to try the same approach the next time. No one else knows what is stressing us. Others cannot see our motivation. The pattern of our responses to stress forms this invisible difference.

Behavior is different than motivation. Behavior is what I do in response to the urging of my motivation. Motivation is invisible. Behavior is visible. It has been common to think of the two as equivalent. They are not. I can easily "fake" my behavior, but not my motivation. As we explore a few of the ways individuals tend to respond to stress, keep in mind the difference between behavior and motivation, the visible and the invisible. Also keep in mind that motivation can change through time. We can learn to choose new patterns. We can choose to respond differently. We can change how our own motivation turns into action.

More than one hundred years ago, psychologists began to recognize how motivation can be "safety-oriented" or "growth-oriented." Safety motivation is primarily expressed through behaviors that are characterized by fear and avoidance.

Growth motivation drives fondness and attraction. Fear most often urges us toward safety motivation; we try to get rid of stress by avoidance. There are also circumstances in which stress performs an enchanting function—it draws us in siren-like fashion to engage and explore.

Stress is highly personal. It is always internal. How we respond to stress may be seen externally, but the stress itself begins internally. The expression of our response to stress is governed by motivation and cannot be seen. Only the resulting behavior can be seen. If we are safety-motivated, our response is fear and avoidance. If we are growth-motivated, our response is to grow and learn.

We as human beings experience inner and outer frames of reference all of the time. These are internal and external. Our consciousness can be attentive to our inner self or it can attend to the world outside of us. The internal is our inner world. Through a complex relationship between physical and mental processes, we experience feelings and emotions.

Traditionally, we have assigned far greater weight to forces outside of us than to those within. The fact of the matter is quite the opposite. It has come as a surprise that while none of us has complete control over all the external conditions of our lives, we have remarkable control over our inner world. This means that when we experience an emotion or feeling, we can relax and make the choice as to how we will allow those emotions and feelings to affect us.

Behaviorists believe that processes like projection or attribution, learning, emotions and feelings are dominantly the product of external stimuli. As we respond to these stimuli, we supposedly enslave ourselves through conditioning. That means that once we establish a pattern of responding to a stimulus, we learn it, and the response rarely wavers after that. Such assumptions provide the foundation for behavioral modification and dominated Western culture's approach to learning and therapy for several hundred years. In this approach, each human is seen as a reservoir of responses that he or she has been conditioned to express.

In marked contrast, more contemporary views shift the responsibility away from the external to the inner workings of humans. The primary contradiction to behaviorism comes from the realization that human beings possess the ability to choose—that is, we can intentionally change our response patterns. Growth comes from repeated opportunities to express control from within, to choose how to respond. All emotions and feelings are inside the person who experiences them, demonstrated both physically and psychologically.

Background about the terms "intrinsic" and "extrinsic" may be helpful. In some ways the terms are similar to the terms "internal locus of control" and "external locus of control" used in psychological literature. In that context, people who tend to exercise an internal locus of control can see cause-and-effect relationships between their behaviors and the results they achieve. This, for example, is a powerful indicator of success in school settings—if I can see that my effort will result in good grades, I will expend the effort.

In contrast, those with an external locus of control see most things as being outside of their control. Things happen to them, not that they can exercise control over what they experience.

Similarly, when people choose to take personal responsibility for values, beliefs and actions, we refer to such people as "intrinsic." Intrinsic people internalize responsibility for motivations and behavior, including behavior in times of stress. In contrast, when people defer responsibility for values, beliefs and actions, we refer to such people as "extrinsic." Extrinsic people externalize responsibility for motivation and behavior.

None of us is perfectly intrinsic at all times. It does help, however, to know the difference. Regularly doing "self checks" is a powerful way to increase one's own awareness of the difference, and increase the time we tend to respond in intrinsic rather than extrinsic ways. For example, remember to check the source of each emotion. The fact is, the source is within each of us—every emotion begins internally. It is too easy to say, "It's your fault," when it couldn't be. It is my choice to respond in whatever way I do.

There are a variety of benefits associated with being intrinsic. Intrinsic people actually tend to experience less stress and demonstrate fewer stress-related health problems than people who tend to externalize stress. Overall, any settings in which people come together to work on problems—in families, neighborhoods, schools, businesses, civic and community settings—tend to be more productive, effective, and successful in collaborative efforts when more people are intrinsic more of the time.

In some cultures, the reflex of generations before us has been to teach us to externalize responsibility for learning, feelings and emotion. We learned to gauge our worth on how things and people outside of ourselves "made us feel." We looked to the outside to determine how to conduct our learning, what emotions to experience, and which feelings to pay attention to. Clearly this is not a plea to ignore the heritage and wisdom of our external culture, but it is a challenge to take the responsibility to go within ourselves to examine the choices we have made. We need the courage to go within to survey those choices that have limited our growth and generosity, those choices that have stunted our spirit. Choice unleashes the human spirit.

Our choices manifest in tendencies when we each are under stress. The results can be seen in five characteristic and different tendencies: Authoritarian, Dependency Manipulative, Intrinsic, Trans Intrinsic and Pan Intrinsic.

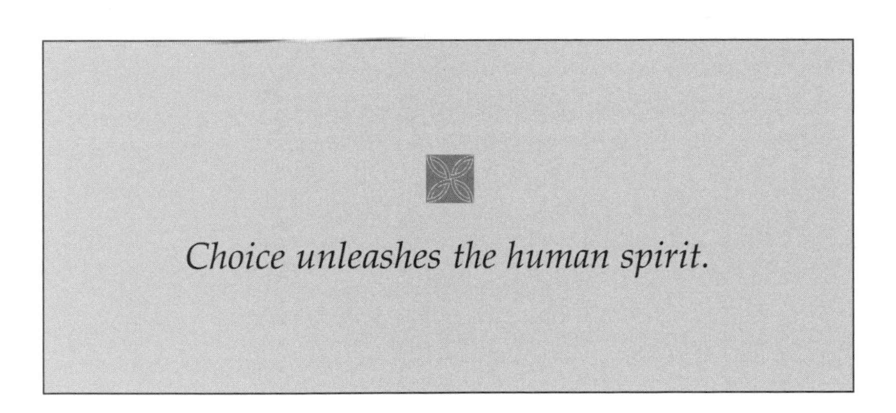

Authoritarian

au thor i tar i an, adjective. favoring complete subjection to authority as opposed to individual freedom. exercising complete or almost complete control over the will of others.

When a person with authoritarian tendencies experiences stress, he or she reflexively goes to an external authority for a safety net. Authoritarians appeal to organized knowledge to provide the content and fact base to demonstrate the rightness of their position. If you do not agree with an Authoritarian, or if you question his or her authority, you are seen as misinformed or stupid. In the view of the Authoritarian, most certainly, you are wrong. The Authoritarian's commitment to "the truth" takes the form of an external relationship. Authoritarians see themselves as representatives of high, distant ideals and truths. The content does not matter. Authoritarians appear as defenders of truth in business, government, arts and child rearing. Authoritarians are prone to require blind obedience to any cause they champion. You are either "with them" or "against them." There is no middle ground. Any questioning of the authority on which they stand is a sacrilege. Such motivational preferences are at the root of the religious and political wars we see in the Middle East, Ireland, Africa and Eastern Europe. These true believers are defending a sacred trust. Authoritarians are safety-motivated. Their belief systems are external to themselves. They want knowledge and truth to be bounded and closed—once you know the truth, you should uphold it and never change it.

The Mirror Image: Anti-Authoritarian

If we were to completely reverse the context in which the Authoritarian works, yet keep the motivation the same, we would be dealing with an Anti-Authoritarian. Anti-Authoritarians are consumed by the external authority that serves the Authoritarian. Under stress, their reflex is to call the truth of others a lie. Just as with Authoritarians, their position is safety-motivated and externally oriented. The will to act is a movement to safety in both cases—one destroys those who question conventional truth, thus achieving safety, and the other reflexively works to destroy conventional truth and its protectors, trying to make the world a safer place from that perspective. With all this destruction, it is difficult to distinguish who is who.

Dependency Manipulative

de pen dence, noun. the state of depending on or needing someone or something for aid.

ma nip u late, verb. 1. to handle, manage, or use. 2. to manage or influence by artful skill. 3. to adapt or change to suit one's own purpose.

The Dependency Manipulative person compulsively needs to belong, to fit into social situations and settings. People with these tendencies are stressed if they feel unwanted, unnecessary or unneeded. At the same time, they develop the skills of manipulation to return the torment by attempting to control or manipulate others. The Dependency Manipulatives are artists of stress. Their media are people and sometimes pets. Some may appear to be aggressive and dominating. Close examination reveals a deep insecurity. Bluster hides the causes of stress. Stress typically comes from loss of control that will affect their self-esteem at a personal level. While Authoritarians look outside themselves for an abstract authority to stand on when stressed, Dependency Manipulatives look to other people to stand on as an external source of affirmation and support. They will often keep others off-balance by making impossible demands. Unrealistic deadlines, excessive requests for immediate action, erratic demands that change from hour to hour are examples of Dependency Manipulative strategies.

Other Dependency Manipulatives step into the role of victim. Their motivation is to force awareness of their victimization on others, winning pity and sympathy. They seek to be exploited in order to feel a strong sense of self-worth and meaning. The meaning comes from the outside, the external, based on their perception of how others respond to them.

Like Authoritarians and Anti-Authoritarians, Dependency Manipulatives are hollow humans. Under stress, they look outside themselves.

Dependency Manipulatives are internally needy. Behaviorally, they may appear to be helpful and attentive. In reality, their lives crisscross time in an endless search for people or situations to exploit, all in an effort to control the emotions and feelings of others as a way to control their perception of their own value.

Intrinsic

in trin sic, adjective. belonging to a thing by its very nature.

Intrinsic motivation is invisible—just as is the motivation of Authoritarians, Anti-Authoritarians and Dependency Manipulatives. The main difference is that people with intrinsic approaches to stress acknowledge that the source of their stress begins within themselves. They internalize, rather than externalize, responsibility for any stress they experience in interaction with ideas or people. They realize they choose to experience, or not experience, stress.

Intrinsics know that they can modify their own patterns of motivation in order to manage, reduce, or eliminate their own stress. As a result, the majority of the stress they experience leads to growth. Novelty, innovation and creativity are core experiences. Every moment of stress is an opportunity to learn. Motivation is an invisible difference among each of these personality types. Intrinsics, however, tend to show less stress and exude more peaceful confidence. They have no need to lash out at others because they know the source of their emotion is inside themselves, and it is up to them to find it and take responsibility for addressing it. In part, their confidence is born of having lost the fear of making mistakes. They are willing to try new options, to embrace them if appropriate and discard them if not.

There are life-changing consequences from accepting and internalizing responsibility for stress rather than externalizing responsibility. If I externalize the sources of my stress, I create a world of "me and them." I develop habits of blaming others and judging others. I defer responsibility. If I give others outside myself the responsibility for controlling my motivation and power over my stress, I can never achieve fulfillment or freedom or true responsibility. My hollowness is complete. In contrast, by internalizing responsibility, I can make conscious choices to control my own stress, my motivation, and my behaviors. My health is enhanced, my effectiveness is increased. In a sense, I have more time and energy to work with others. Instead of blaming others, I support others—beginning within myself.

Trans Intrinsic

The Trans Intrinsic grows from the concept of trans, meaning to cross or connect. This is the Intrinsic person who commits to serving and experiencing other people in his or her life work. The first characteristic of such people is an internalized response to stress. The second characteristic is that such people internalize responsibility for their own beliefs and behaviors while simultaneously living in service to others. They cross a line from self to others, carrying the tendency to internalize responsibility in this transit. Being Intrinsic, they do not externalize their beliefs in an abstract code of ethics. Nor are they prone to manipulating or being dependent on others. They do care deeply about others, however. They have powerful convictions. The difference is that they take responsibility for their beliefs and actions. They then transport their commitments into a world of service to others.

Pan Intrinsic

Pan Intrinsic people explore issues of global proportion. Pan, as we use the term here, means embracing all. Pan Intrinsic people take responsibility for their beliefs, actions, stresses and motivations while they simultaneously focus on the greater good. Their scope spans concerns for individual animals to whole species, individual children to all of lifekind. Sometimes, it is possible to confuse Authoritarians for Pan Intrinsics. Looking more closely, the confusion disappears. Authoritarians tend to tell us what to think and why we must think it, and, if stressed, will revert to authorities outside themselves such as dogma for support. The Pan Intrinsic holds concerns just as deeply, but begins by internalizing his or her conviction. Pan Intrinsics explore issues of great consequence. World hunger, the origins of poverty, spiritual well-being, the meaning of community—these are all examples. They want to improve the condition of all forms of life through their many ways of serving. All the Intrinsics emanate a peaceful spirit. The differences among Intrinsics are about scale, not motivation.

Activity: Stress Reflection

In your journal, make two columns. Title the first "internal" and the second "external." Each time throughout the day that you find yourself experiencing stress, put the time in one column or the other with one or two words to remind you of the circumstance. Typically, as time passes and you practice this art of stress reflection, you will have more and more notes in the internal column, and you will have fewer and fewer moments of stress in any given day.

List 10 values that are most important to you. Reflect on each. Determine which you hold because of your own conscious choices and which, if any, you hold—perhaps unconsciously—as a result of external influences. Some may clearly be a combination of both.

Autonomy, Affiliation, Acceptance and Agreement

> *One of the signs of a healthy civilization is the existence of a relatively clear language in which everyone can participate in their own way.*
>
> John Ralston Saul

au ton o my, noun. independence or freedom, as of the will, one's actions.

af fil i ate, verb. 1. to bring into close association or connection. 2. to attach or unite in terms of fellowship, associate.

This section explores the significance of a variety of concepts as they relate to ideas of creativity and community. The concepts are relevant to nurturing the intrinsic. The intrinsic, in turn, is a fundamental enabler of healthy communities.

We have heard passionate arguments voicing fear about how the quest for autonomy, seen as individualism, is contributing to the destruction of community. Proponents of this view equate autonomy with selfishness. After all, they argue, how can you be community-oriented if you are off on a quest for self-fulfillment? To be virtuous, the group-oriented voice claims, community should be based on mutualism and service.

While this is true, it is important to remember that few healthy communities are populated with people who are spiritually and morally hollow. A certain amount of self-reliance and self-regulation must be among the skills one brings to community. Attending to the development of these inner strengths increases the likelihood that a community member will exercise his or her creativity and authentically contribute to the whole. Consider the opposite. Hollow humans bring only spiritual neediness—they appear as parasites or predators, drawing upon the community's strengths and resources as they attempt to gain what they do not have.

Many autonomous people choose to serve in communities. Those without the strength of autonomy affiliate out of guilt, neediness and dependence. Such motivating qualities never serve the best in community. Clearly, autonomy also can have a dark side if it is based on greed, selfishness and narcissism. However, to ignore its strengths is to toss the possibility out with the bath water.

Healthy autonomy is graced by individuals who practice their personal creativity and choose to serve the community rather than being coerced or ordered to do so. Healthy autonomy produces healthy affiliation because it brings with it humans who choose from a place of willing contribution. People who choose creativity and commitment from a base of personal fulfillment are rich with useful contributions. Hollowness serves the despot, restricts creativity and limits the life of community. Hollowness—within individuals and within whole communities—is job security for despots.

Healthy affiliation lacks coercion and manipulation. It creates interrelatedness out of interdependence. Strangely, many use the word interdependence as a metaphor for health in natural and cultural communities. Whenever we hear it used repeatedly, we suspect that there may be the ghost of manipulative control lurking at the edges of what the speaker is saying. Interrelatedness and interconnections are power neutral. Interdependence adds power to the equation and raises the political ante.

Those who fear that autonomous people threaten and dismantle community are generally wrong. First is the assumption that autonomy breeds selfishness, the will to exploit others for personal gain. Autonomy is popularly attributed to those who are cavalierly self-serving and out for themselves. Some misguided proponents of community feel that autonomy is bonded to the negative side of rugged individualism, a condition they see as anti-community. In this case, autonomy is equated with a dangerous and unpredictable selfishness.

If selfishness is exploitative, some would say that its opposite, selflessness, is not. On closer examination, selflessness can be exploitative as well. Selfless people often exploit themselves for the benefit of others. Such self-exploitation results in a tendency to be all things to all people, a surefire formula for burnout. If they don't burn out, those people who compulsively give to others often pack their lives so full of others' demands that they do not find time for their own growth. They effectively stop learning.

Consider the anguished corporate achiever who discovers at forty that he or she has been giving to a career for more than 20 years. As this person reaches within, he or she finds a tangle of habits and reflexes that have worn with time. There is no newness, no capacity for innovation. Just as the selfish find little of their own making within their souls, only the treasures they steal from others, the selfless may find hollowness born of giving without receiving.

Balance is forged of giving and receiving in spiritually equal portions. We use the term "selfness" as a way to characterize this condition of balance. Selfness is a basic skill for healthy autonomy. It is a close relative of the intrinsic tendency to take personal responsibility for values, beliefs and actions. Selfness honors an authentic balance of giving to and taking from self and others. It avoids the take-until-they-are-empty-style of the selfish, and the give-until-I-drop style of the selfless. Selfness allows us to transcend the either/or implications of give and take. Selfness achieves a healthy balance in which autonomous individuals choose affiliation.

The result is healthy individuals, expressing personal if not public creativity, living in healthy communities.

On reflection, even the words "give and take" are somewhat harsh. Giving can be as aggressive as taking if there are expectations woven into the act. For example, if I give you a gift—a piece of jewelry—and then scan you every time we meet to see if you are wearing it, it is a gift with a price. In effect, my expectation is that if I give you a gift, you will certainly wear it. This makes the present less a gift and more an obligation. It is easy to see how, in this case, the giving of a gift—an apparently selfless act—is in reality a selfish act swaddled in a cloak of manipulation.

In the condition we call selfness, a gift is given out of generosity rather than manipulation. The act is intrinsic. In selfness, a gift is received without obligation and expectation. In contrast, one acquaintance of ours often gives books as gifts. It takes no time at all to discover that these gifts are required reading. We are expected to find a particular message in each book that is to be incorporated somehow in the fabric of our relationship. There was always a touch of hurt when we disclosed that we had not gotten around to reading the book or, worse yet, found it not particularly valuable or interesting. That kind of gift is an expression of a form of selfishness, tied to a desire to control, not a manifestation of the intrinsic.

Both selfishness and selflessness in their exploitative form have the capacity for harboring expectations within the framework of giving and taking. In selfness, the giving and taking become more like offering and accepting.

The acts of offering and accepting have energy and direction but the surrounding expectations are lower than in classic forms of give-and-take.

ac cept ance, noun. 1. the act of taking or receiving something offered. 2. favorable reception; approval; favor.

a gree ment, noun. unanimity of opinion; harmony in feeling.

Bob tells this story:

> *In the past, some of my most troublesome moments have occurred when I harbored the notion that accepting something was the same thing as agreeing with something or someone. Painfully, I have found this to be untrue. Due to my university education, and especially my training in the natural sciences, I came to believe that discourse ended whenever everyone reached a state of logical, rational agreement. This was an illusion. I also suffered under the illusion that when rational agreement occurred, all involved would tremble in awe and enter the sacred domain of truth. Truth is what reason produces. For some time, I considered agreement and acceptance to be the same thing. If I agreed with you, I accepted you. If you agreed with me, you accepted me. I somehow missed the point that, taken to an extreme, this is a perfect formula for racism, sexism, and all the other "isms" that produce separation.*

I learned how easy it is to accept people with whom I agree and how difficult it is to accept those who disagree with me. This awareness rocked me into the realization that I was intentionally ignoring people who disagreed with me and, by doing so, I was cutting off a viable path for personal growth and community health. I had created a pattern that nourished in-group/out-group relationships. I was stifling my own growth by insulating myself from ideas contrary to mine. Even more insidious, I was destroying opportunities for my friends and others to grow as well. Nothing stops thought as quickly as agreement. Community, if it emerges at all in such settings, is born with potentially serious defects.

Let me provide an example. During the early 1970s, I was director of some projects funded through the National Science Foundation. The task was to create classroom assignments that furthered student knowledge and skills in learning science. Much of the work was conducted in 12 major cities nationwide. Each had inner-city schools with largely African-American student populations. Our job was to test the viability of our project materials by teaching the trial units in inner-city classrooms in these cities.

The atmosphere I found in each classroom I entered was sullen and hostile. I was surprised by the lack of acceptance I felt. Bewilderment welled inside me. I sensed I was experiencing racism in action.

Knowing well my own motives and intent, I resented being treated in such a manner.

Students glowered and mumbled about me to each other. Like a voice spoken from a great distance, I heard myself saying, "Come on class. Cool it and you can see what a nice guy I am." I grinned at them but received no returning warmth. One student said, "Man, all honkies start out by tellin' you how nice they are then your face see the floor up close with some white guy beatin' your ass." I looked at the teacher and found little support. He had seen this before. His expression told me that he also wanted to find out "what kind of honky I was."

I picked up a Polaroid camera and muttered that we would be going outside in groups and photographing evidence of change. The silence that followed my nervous comment heightened the sense of non-communication. It became clear that I had received some positive points by skipping the typical white adult teacher's response to the swearing. By not mentioning it and moving on, combined with the seductive promise of going outside with a camera, I gained a temporary glimpse of acceptance. This was acceptance, to this point, without agreement. The rest of the lesson, and growth experience for me, went very well. The students did all the things that students do. They argued, bantered, and gave each other unwanted and wanted advice.

They tossed the developer papers on the school grounds (these were early Polaroids) and ignored them until they saw me picking them up. Then, after a whispered discussion, each group started picking up the trash they had created.

The students carried out this assignment as effectively as any group I had seen. Back in the classroom, they boisterously showed each other their results. They developed and discussed insights into the content of the lesson. I made some headway as well. The student who first hassled me asked if I would return tomorrow. He seemed surprised when I said I would be with them all week. "All right," he said. "Most honkies spend an hour and then disappear." As I left the school at the end of the day, after working with six different classrooms of students, I noticed that there were no film wrappers outside—although the grounds were crusted with litter overall.

That day remains vivid in my memory. I think about what it taught me about the concept of community and the roles of acceptance and agreement as they relate to values and beliefs. I discovered that I could make far more progress as an educator by admitting that I am a racist than I could by trying to deny it. It was difficult for me during the emerging drama of the civil-rights movement in the 1970s to admit that if the children saw me as a racist, I was a racist.

It was clear that all the noble reasons, constructed and footnoted in my mind, were of no use to youth who looked up and saw a white male adult telling them how to live their lives so that his whiteness would be comfortable. Ironically, the racist in this description might just as easily be a sexist or an ageist. While I cannot do much to change what I am, I can control what I do with the package I was born with. This is the foundation for growth in the realms of both autonomy and affiliation. The key is empathy.

To maintain healthy communities, we need acceptance and agreement, unity and differences. When the children in class saw me as an oppressor, they drew on their past experiences with racism. It was a mistake on my part not to see that every experience is a new one. When I took offense at the students for not seeing my intentions, I performed an act of racism. Intentions cannot be seen, they must be experienced. Whatever I did was done by an adult, white male teacher in power. Whatever they did was done by young black students with very little power.

When I shift from judgment and power to acceptance and respect, the impact of racism is diminished. The impact is diminished but it does not disappear. I am still white, male and adult—all attributes of people of power in this culture. If I want to limit the negative effects of racism in my community, I must accept that I am perceived by some as racist.

I must accept that perception and demonstrate with my actions that I am attempting to behave with authenticity and in a healing fashion. If I can demonstrate acceptance of myself and others, I may be able to move toward acceptance and agreement with integrity. If we can create communities of acceptance, where there is room for agreement and disagreement, we can transcend racism and the other forces that divide us as humans.

Acceptance means I recognize that I view every other person through my own stereotypes and conclusions. Acceptance means I recognize my limitations and I work to accept others for exactly who, what and how they are. Performing the act of acceptance puts us in direct contact with the mind and soul of whomever we accept. Once accepted, a person enters the relationship less vulnerable to judgment. Acceptance suspends judgment. With suspended judgment, I can hear you as you are rather than how I want you to be. Acceptance creates the opportunity for us to greet each other as worthy individuals with different experiences.

We can strongly disagree with one another in environments of acceptance. Acceptance does not necessarily mean agreement. The point is not necessarily to agree, or not. What is valuable and important to the health of individuals and of communities is to be able to sort out the differences in furthering ways. Acceptance allows each person to be authentic, and to be perceived as authentic.

Acceptance allows for genuine resolution of differences through collaboration in an environment of mutual respect.

Bob tells another story:

> *Communities are said to be based upon trust. But what does trust actually mean? A friend and I were in conversation when her daughter announced that she was going out and would be taking her mother's car. My friend called out, "Have a good time and remember, I trust you." Once the daughter was gone, I asked my friend what she meant by trust. She looked blankly at me and admitted that the phrase had gotten to be like a verbal peck on the cheek; it was a reflex. It ranked alongside the phrase, "I am glad you liked it," in reply to a guest who remarked that she enjoyed a meal, or, "How are you?" and "Fine."*
>
> *She puzzled. "I guess it means that she will behave in ways that I would approve of." I asked if she could possibly mean something like, "I expect you will behave in ways that will please you." "Oh no," she shrieked, "I want her to behave in ways that will please me."*

Individuals, families, businesses and communities experience a great deal of confusion about the concept of trust.

Young people want the limits of trust to be established as part of their own autonomy and integrity. They want the authority to choose to behave in ways that express the core qualities of the person they are trying to become. Families, businesses and communities prefer to establish the criteria for trust. This circumstance creates one of the most volatile flash points in human relationships—which clash between the internal needs of individuals and the conserving needs of families, businesses, communities and other institutions. Trust weighs heavily in these environments.

The rules of conduct central to community values are often called to the surface when stress occurs. Young people often create such stresses and the community must respond. Bob describes this circumstance:

> *Several years ago I asked a tribal friend of mine what the greatest source of stress for young people on the reservation was. Instantly he answered, "MTV!" He went on to say that no one had anticipated how exposure to rock music videos would flood traditional tribal values with radical contemporary alternatives. Whatever previously constituted trust had to be reexamined. Core values of community were in conflict with the will to change. "I trust you to be a complete expression of what and who you are" was positioned in conflict with "I trust you to forget the new ways and behave in ways consistent with tradition as I interpret it for you."*

Acceptance does not necessarily mean agreement. Trust means both options have validity. In fact, they may not be mutually exclusive. In an atmosphere of respect and dignity, which grows from acceptance, there is spiritual protection for those who differ. There is a basic honoring of the notion that both maturation and integrity grow from honoring the individual choice as well as community needs. That which nourishes the individual will also serve the common good. Trust to nurture the self inevitably nourishes the trust the community extends to all.

If such an atmosphere prevails—and it did in this tribal community—both conditions are met. After several Native American Indian rock bands formed, the tribal elders were pleased to find that the lyrical content for many of the songs extended traditional values to audiences unfamiliar with this inclusive world view.

Acceptance
does not necessarily
mean agreement.

Activity: Expectation Traps

Make a list of expectations that others have of you that you feel they have no right to have of you.

Make a list of expectations that you have of others. Check yourself to identify your intent with each expectation—whether it is to limit or support yourself, the other person or both of you.

Define the differences and similarities between each of the following:
Manipulating and helping.
Giving and offering.
Taking and accepting.
Accepting and agreeing.

Explore the following in your mind and write a few notes in your journal about each statement:
Acceptance does not mean expectation.
Agreement means expectation.
Judgment is fundamental to agreement.
Experience is fundamental to acceptance.

Check your tendency to use the word "trust" as a metaphor for control.

Write in your journal about how you feel when someone else says he or she trusts you, and how you feel when you say "I trust you" to another. Consider the similarities and differences between trust and expectation.

Capacity, Action and Aspiration

> *Community might seem a strange word to use in conjunction with the ever-expanding virtual world. But one of my most robust findings about e-culture is that it centers around strong communities, online and off. The community-forming potential of the Web presents both the greatest opportunity and the greatest threat to organizations.*
>
> Rosabeth Moss Kanter
> *Evolve!*

ca pa cit y, noun. actual or potential ability to perform.

action, noun. something performed; an act; deed.

as pi rat ion, noun. strong desire, longing or aim.

Capacity is what I am capable of becoming. Action is how I guide my capacity to become. Aspiration is what I dream of becoming. Self-actualization, as described by Abraham Maslow, is the condition that emerges when all of these qualities are in balance. A guiding premise throughout this book is that healthy communities are composed of healthy individuals. We celebrate the differences among us, and the capacities and dreams of each. We look for ways to have individuals of all ages develop their own capacities and aspirations. One of the ways to do so is by taking action and learning from the results.

Capacity

Some of us were born to walk on the moon, others to write sonnets about it. A hundred other possibilities could be listed here, each an expression of the human capacities we possess. All of these options have the potential to be superior expressions of what we choose to do in the world. Our basic human design has provided us with countless ways to choose an endeavor and see it through. Basic to our capacities is the ability to learn knowledge and skills. However, specific content and skills are not enough to provide complete fulfillment. Our choices must have integrity and authenticity. As humans, we have among us, and within us, a yearning and a capacity to contribute to the common good.

Earlier, when we explored the concepts of autonomy and affiliation, we argued the need for intrinsic, autonomous fulfillment while individuals engage in the quest for service through affiliation. Such approaches contribute to the likelihood that individual—and therefore community—capacity will be fulfilled effectively, constructively and creatively.

One of the most common reflexes of contemporary times is to assume that unless you are doing something, you cannot be making a contribution. T-shirts exhort us, "Don't just stand there. Do something!" People at meetings erupt in frustration with, "I am tired of talking about it. We have got to do something!" Popular clothing advertisements shout, "Just do it." And, some grandparents still warn, "The devil finds work for idle hands."

The secret to effective action is to keep it in alignment with capacities. If there is a gap in alignment, each of us has the opportunity to establish realignment by acquiring skills and knowledge. Western thinkers are prone to think of learning in terms of changes in behavior, with behavior as the action part of the formula. If we choose to learn something that changes our behavior, then the advocates of visible action are sated.

There is an alternative T-shirt. It says, "Don't just do something. Stand there!" It is difficult for us to accept the fact that reflection is the behavior we cannot see. So too it is with other forms of thought such as meditation, prayer, reverie and all the forms of dreaming. It is in the reflective ways of thinking that we do so much to nourish our inner capacities, those capacities that provide strength in autonomy. Action can be and often is oversold. We have plenty of evidence that many of the Earth's ills as well as problems at all scales of human activity—in individuals, families, businesses, communities and nations—are the result of actions without reflection.

Reflective ways of thinking
nourish our inner capacities.
Many of Earth's ills are the result of
action without reflection.

There is subtle interplay between capacity, action and reflection. Many serious thinkers in this time of massive transformation in world society suggest another context in which to frame our thinking. This new emphasis is embraced by the concept of becoming. It is common, when action is overemphasized, to oversell doing as well. Doing, after all, is a manifestation of action. You can see what we can do. Learning theory tells us that when I am stimulated, I respond. That response is the doing. The danger of all this is that it can easily get me to focus on what I can do when I learn something rather than what I am becoming because of what I have learned.

Becoming embraces capacities and how they are added to and change. Becoming guides the action or nonaction I take. Becoming is choreographed by my aspiration—my soul flying toward the future.

Aspiration is what we hope to become. It is more than a plan and more than a goal. What we aspire to is the spiritual destination of the process of becoming. It is always vague and framed more in metaphor than in specific deeds and accomplishments. It is the willful way we as humans enter into the process of evolution. Contrast these postures:

> "I want to go to college, get a good job, marry the love of my life, raise a family, and retire solvent at the age of 65."

> "I want to learn interesting and useful things, help create a vital life with family and friends, share a life that fulfills us, and make a contribution to the well-being of life on Earth."

Both are valid approaches and are not mutually exclusive. The first has a stronger plan of action embedded in it. It is consistent with traditional community values. The second approach has greater ambiguity and subjectivity. Leaving room for unpredictability opens the door to innovation. The second approach considers ambiguity an asset.

Leaving room for unpredictability opens the door to innovation.

Once again, balance is the key. Warren Weaver, a mathematician, once said, "We must educate our young so that they grow up to be fearless in the face of the tentative." Certainty is embedded in nostalgia as we peer toward the future. As an individual, if I attempt to hone useful skills for community life, I must gain comfort with ambiguity. This means that I must view my capacities as evolutionary. I must be willing to dance with change. The actions I take in the name of community must be born of both action and reflection. My aspirations must embrace new and emerging solutions. I must focus on becoming rather than having become. Becoming is an open-system concept. Having become is closed, complete, finished.

Activity: Personal Portrait

List ten things that many people think you are good at but in reality you know you can significantly improve. Examine the list and identify those you can actively improve with specific knowledge and skills. Look at the list again and put a check mark by those things you want to be good at and draw a line through those you don't care about being good at. Make a plan to work on those you want to be good at.

Take three "time-outs" a day—each time to simply reflect on the actions you have taken since the last time you paused to reflect.

Cultivate the habit of "quiet time," in which you celebrate the silence around you. Check the tendency to pile action upon action without reflecting on the results. Looking for results is another form of action.

Consider doing nothing for nothing's sake, because of the inherent value of nourishing yourself in peaceful ways.

Create a personal portrait. In three areas of your picture of yourself, create images of your capacities, your actions and your aspirations.

Create an outer circle of reflection as a way to keep the image in balance. Look to see what you have achieved in each area, and where you want to develop yourself more.

The Power of Prejudice

> *As nature continues its game of biological mutation and selection, and as humans play their own games of selection of ideas and of cultural innovations, nature will have the last word.*
>
> Jonas Salk
> *Survival of the Wisest*

It is important to recognize that prejudice has both negative and positive attributes. For our purposes here, negative prejudice is unwarranted and inflexible negative regard for someone or something. Positive prejudice is unwarranted and inflexible positive regard for someone or something.

When I express a negative prejudice, I have expectations that whomever the prejudice is directed at will behave in a way I find aggravating and contrary to my beliefs. Somehow, I will designate the target as humanly unworthy. It may appear as a negative expectation about intellect, feelings, demeanor, skills, taste, manners and so on. The list is endless.

Prejudice is frequently institutionalized in communities. That is, communities tend to formalize who is considered acceptable and who is not, what behavior is acceptable and what is not. The core of prejudicial beliefs is passed on through family, schools, religion, government, business, politics and art. In nearly all cultures, there are beliefs about race, gender, age, ethnicity, religion and other attributes that provide the basis for reflexively rejecting another's worth or status. This rejection is generally accepted within a culture as appropriate.

Prejudice is at the core of some of the most profound human ills that we experience. It is at the root of racism, sexism, ageism, adultism and many other reflexive judgments that are involved in creating intellectual and emotional distance between ourselves and others. Perceived superiority is a close companion to such prejudice. Each object of prejudice is seen as inferior to the one who exercises the prejudice.

We can reduce and eliminate most negative prejudice from our lives at a personal level. Starting within ourselves as individuals is the way to begin to address prejudice within communities.

Many times we overlook the fact that negative prejudice places limits on our own growth as individuals. Any time I demonstrate negative prejudice, I have relegated the object of my prejudice to a closed system. My mind is made up. I will explore the concept no more. Prejudice is the mind's way of closing down the ability to explore options through intellect, emotions and feelings.

One of the most fertile areas for examining prejudice is in the relationships between children and adults. The prejudices we have about the limits of children's abilities form the foundation of adultism. Adultism is the way anyone who has reached adult status may exercise control over children's capacities, actions and aspirations.

Children are often victimized by adults through the years prior to their adolescence. This victimization takes place in the indiscriminate ways that adults exert power over children. Even well-meaning parents are sometimes intractable in the ways they demand obedience. This is not to say that obedience itself should be abandoned. After all, personal safety and civility require obedience. Playing on the freeway and hitting another child with a baseball bat are behaviors we must control. Yet too often there is no time taken after enforcing obedience through a reprimand, a shout, a slap on the buttocks, or an insult to let the child understand the rationale for the action that was taken.

What most children remember about how power is exerted is their own helplessness in the face of a unilateral demand for obedience. They store resentment and futility in childhood's powerlessness. This overflows when they feel the growing persistence of puberty. They then sense a terrifying liberation born on waves of equity denied. Nothing parents or guardians can do will suppress their passage into adulthood, in spite of how they may lack experience or readiness for their own power at that time. Adultism is brought to justice during adolescence. For a brief or perhaps eternal moment, adolescents respond fully to the history of oppression they experienced as children. Many seem to feel that any adult they come in contact with is responsible for the injustices they have felt. The youth mete out revenge. These are classic responses for having suffered adultism. It is during this period that many adults respond with their own pattern of fear—avoiding as much as possible any meaningful contact with teenagers.

Adultism takes many forms. It is empowered by society's bequest of authority on adults to control and manage all that children experience. On command, children play the violin for Aunt Minnie, leave the television to take out the garbage, answer questions in school without having a choice, and more.

As trivial as these examples are, they represent the seedbeds for prejudice being tilled. It is well known that abused children are more likely to become abusers than non-abused children. Children who experience excessive adultism are likely to exert similarly unwarranted power over children when they become adults. As children grow and their body size fades into the adult world, they lose the consciousness and conspicuousness of children. Gender and skin color remain with them as do a host of invisible differences.

Prejudice is the mind's way of closing down the ability to explore options.

Hundreds of scholarly studies through time have addressed the turbulence of adolescence. Each book on the topic, each town meeting, proposes a list of factors that contribute to the dissonance. The adolescent years are a time of turmoil during which young adults try to reconstruct the dignity they lost during childhood. In the process, as they suffer the further humiliation of being rejected again, confusion overwhelms them. Bell Hooks in her book, *Killing Rage: Ending Racism,* points out that middle-class blacks, who have achieved economic equity, still experience rage against the system that has come to embrace them. Rage is born of the feeling that they have sold out to the very system that forged the oppression in the first place.

Rage characterizes the intellect, emotions and feelings of humans who respond to prejudice. A fire in the soul demands freedom. Prejudice descends as a falling cloak of oppression. It comes down from those who presume superiority to those whom they presume inferior. Lifting the cloak reveals hierarchy, shedding the cloak requires equity. If we choose to cast prejudice aside, we are making a choice that involves both freedom and justice. Inner freedom from negative prejudice may be the ultimate form of justice among humans. Prejudice can be swallowed by open-minded freedom.

Positive prejudice can be as oppressive as negative prejudice. It simply takes longer to discover it, and we consciously cherish some of its effects. A positive prejudice can be seen as a value in the context of communities. A value is a prejudice that is approved of culturally. A positive prejudice is a value we hold favorably.

Love is a form of positive prejudice. In the early stages of romantic love, two people may feel the blush of perceived perfection surrounding them. Unwarranted positive prejudice permeates the air. Such positive prejudice often leads to expectation. Expectation is one of the parents of prejudice. I subtly construct a list of how you should behave in order to continue to manifest all the things about you that I consider perfect. Tacit lists of expectations grow to implicit contracts. Soon the list of expectations grows from the personal to the public arena. Now we configure our choices into expectations and they constitute the boundaries of a relationship that has become a mini-institution. Positive prejudice can become as confining as negative prejudice. Consider how you feel if someone constantly touts your virtues beyond what you think is accurate or realistic. Some of the feeling is pleasant, and can even serve as an inspiration. Then there is the feeling of fear of being discovered as less than what is being described. Then there is anger about being misrepresented. Even positive prejudice has its downside.

For children, positive prejudice sets up failure more than negative prejudice does. The overindulgent parent informs the whole family, if not the neighborhood and all the family, of your perfection. You are sent to bed each night with your stomach churning in fear—fear that maybe tomorrow you will fail and be discovered. That leads to the double bind of not wanting to fail yourself and not wanting to fail the parent who seems to bask in your perfection.

By definition, a prejudice is an unwarranted opinion about something or someone.

Prejudice is carefully constructed and rests on an elaborate rationale: Children should be seen and not heard; the urban poor would rather be on welfare than work; all immigrants should speak English if they move here; women are too emotional to be effective in positions of leadership. In the minds of those who harbor and use prejudice negatively, their stance is completely warranted. Reason is not reason when it limits the human mind and soul.

Activity: Probing Prejudice

Make a list of positive and negative prejudices that your parents demonstrated.

List instances in which you were victimized by prejudice: as a child, because of your gender, because of your skin color, due to your beliefs, because of your body, because of your age.

Listen to the jokes you tell and the jokes you hear others tell. Analyze the jokes for the extent to which their humor depends on prejudice—positive or negative.

List examples from your own life when you have experienced positive prejudice. Reflect on the pluses and minuses associated with the experience.

What is the overall effect of both positive and negative prejudice in your own life? Describe how they have affected you personally.

The Power Of Words

The power to tell our own story about who we are and who we might become is one of our least-acknowledged powers.

Betty Sue Flowers
Poet, Author, Educator, Futurist

Through the years, we have found the following guidelines to be an enormously helpful tool. These simple suggestions serve to nourish the intrinsic while making oneself deeply aware of the power of words. Each is a way to assist oneself in being self-reflective and aware of the impact of our choice of words on our own effectiveness in a community. Some are more difficult than others. None has to be done all the time. Read the list. We follow the list with an additional explanation and rationale for some of the most difficult. Cheryl is reminded of a day many years ago—in the 1970s—when she first made the effort to consciously state "he or she" in a sentence, rather than the traditional use of the male pronoun. Around that time we found a term coined by the psychologist, Albert Ellis, who practiced and encouraged what he called "semantitherapy." It works. For us, the notion is to pay attention to the words we choose and use—and, by practicing this greater awareness, the results are not only personally therapeutic but societally as well.

Speak in the first person, active voice. This is a way to use language to indicate personal responsibility. That is, "I believe…" rather than "We believe…"

Speak in the declarative. That means avoid asking questions. Questions put people on the defensive. To ask a question is an act of exercising power. I limit the options of the person to whom I am speaking because my question is a way to limit the topics we will discuss. Often we ask questions genuinely to be data seeking; however, the act of questioning remains an act of power. When you do ask questions, notice the circumstances in which you ask them—and the frequency.

Avoid asking "Why?" questions. All questions are invasive. Why questions in particular are limiting and difficult. A why question requires a rationale, a reason, to be provided. Justification is being sought. Often, we put people on the defensive when we ask why— "Why did you do that?"

Check the tendency to say, "Yes, but…" rather than "Yes, and . . ." "And" allows you to take an idea in another direction without contradicting or polarizing the perspective of the person with whom you are speaking. "Yes, but" tends to be competitive. "Yes, and" tends to be collaborative.

Avoid the tendency to scapegoat. "It is her fault;" or "I only did that because of the way I was raised;" or . . . You get the picture.

Pay attention to gender in language. Be gender fair. As a culture, we are much better at using both male and female pronouns than we used to be. It is still the case that use of the male pronoun to refer to both men and women is denigrating and limiting to human females. Going to the trouble of saying "he or she," rather than using the male pronoun alone, makes a big difference to the listener—and the speaker—in terms of conveying and practicing the arts of respectful communication.

Use metaphors from nature. Natural metaphors convey life. They hold within the power of renewal and generation. They are nourishing. Contrast natural metaphors with mechanical metaphors or, worse, war metaphors. The results are profoundly different. The first are healing; the second and third are inherently limiting and, at times, destructive.

Avoid the tendency to make evaluative statements. Making judgments is a human tendency. At the same time, the results are limiting when applied to another human. Often we think our choice to say, "That's great," is supportive. It can be; at the same time, the act of making such statements leaves everything else less than great. Judgments are comparisons. There is a place for them—just not with as much frequency as we tend to use them in contemporary culture.

Check the source of each emotion. We said this earlier. The point is to remember—even at moments of great stress—that the choice is ours. The emotion always begins within each of us. Nothing is more personal, more intimate, more your own.

Speaking Personally: I and We

I, pronoun, singular. the nominative singular pronoun used by a speaker in referring to himself or herself.

we, pronoun, plural. used by a speaker or writer to denote one's self and another person or persons.

One of the tricks we let culture play on us has to do with politeness—especially in the form of some everyday courtesies.

Bob tells this story:

> *My mother doted on politeness. As a single parent, she enforced any lapse in manners with sudden and lasting reminders. One of her pet peeves involved the use of the word "I." She maintained that people who used "I" too much were selfish, egotistical, self-centered and filled with their own self-importance. They should be avoided. It did not occur to her that speaking in the first person is a way to take personal responsibility for beliefs. As a result, I avoided saying things like, "I believe . . ."*
>
> *It became a hard habit to break in the years that followed. Sentences rolled easily off my tongue using the polite "we": "It looks like we have had enough of this," or "What we need right now is some exercise."*

I came to realize that in my effort to obey my mother I slipped into speech patterns that avoided any personal responsibility for what I said. The imperial "we," "us" and "our" made anything I was saying seem to imply an unspoken consensus among whomever was present. Such inclusion without permission is, as I later concluded, rude, manipulative or both. Perhaps worse, it subtly teaches a form of externalizing rather than internalizing responsibility for personal beliefs and desires.

In the past few decades, the advent of new forms of group therapy and decision-making did restore the use of the "I." The argument was that we, as a culture, had lapsed into avoiding responsibility for what we said and did. To get us back on track, such gatherings made it a house rule to speak in the first person. "We don't know what you mean" became "I don't know what you mean."

We go further and recommend that statements be made in the first person and the declarative. This too can be taken to the extreme. We simply encourage checking the tendency to defer responsibility by word choice. Speaking in the first person tends to cultivate clear expressions of personal responsibility. Speaking in the first person and the declarative reinforces our tendency to be intrinsic.

If speaking in the first person is difficult, our suggestion to speak in the first person and the declarative is even more difficult. Speak in the declarative. What does that mean? It means avoid the tendency to ask questions. Few people in most cultures are aware of the exaggerated role of questioning in the way we talk with each other.

Consider this scene:

It is Saturday morning in the supermarket. A mother with a three-year-old meets a longtime friend she seldom sees. After preliminary greetings, the friend focuses on the child. "Hi, dear. What's your name? How old are you? Are you in school? What grade are you in? Do you have any brothers and sisters?"

We adults tend to think we are displaying friendly interest by taking such an approach when talking with children. The results, however, are powerfully disempowering. If I ask a question, I have the power. I am forcing a response and, typically, a narrow response because, out of the universe of topics we could discuss, I have predetermined what is important. Children learn the ground rules quickly. In contrast, next time you meet a small child, start a conversation about something of interest to you that you think might be of interest to the child as well. The results are usually profoundly different than what happens in response to the typical interrogation at the market described above. Questions usually yield monosyllabic responses from children. Declarative statements often yield sentences and even whole paragraphs!

In school settings, similar questioning styles dominate. As much as 90 percent of instructional time is dominated by questioning strategies. Texts and other instructional materials, under the guise of inquiry, are packed with questions. Often when teachers ask a question and there is no response, they ask another and another. Mary Budd Rowe, a respected scholar, discovered that when teachers ask an unsuccessful question, they wait as little as two seconds before asking another question to clarify the first. Under this aggressive pattern of repetitive questioning, children answer in short sentences and abrupt phrases. It isn't just a lapse in content that the students experience. They are psychologically put on the defensive. The urgency and aggression can strongly affect their self-esteem. Rowe's research showed that if a question were followed by five to seven seconds of wait time, students tended to speak in complete sentences and long commentary.

A Navajo man we once knew chastised us and our European-American kin when he said, "You white people, you bring a weapon wrapped in the songs of your speech. It is the question. You think you can use it any time you want to destroy my people's silence. A question shatters my silence." It was informing and important to us to discover that languages of many primal peoples in the Americas and other parts of the world did not use questions, the interrogative, until Europeans arrived.

Activity: Practicing Speech in the First Person

Speak in the first person. Build a reflex to say "I believe" as a way to demonstrate your personal acknowledgment of responsibility for the statements you make and the beliefs you hold.

Speak in the declarative. Enter into conversation by exposing what you know or do not know. Try to go through an entire conversation at a meal or a party without asking a question of another.

Speak in the first person and the declarative at the same time. "I would love to know if you have read any good books lately. I have read a few."

Keep a journal page reflecting all the questions asked of you, and your responses, throughout a single day. If one day involves too many questions, start with one hour!

At a business meeting, track the use of "we," "us" and "our" versus "I." Look for any patterns of manipulation, scapegoating, deferring responsibility or internalizing responsibility.

Start a conversation with a child without asking any questions. Compare the results to those times when you began a conversation with, "How old are you? Where do you go to school?"

More About Questions and Questioning

ques tion, noun. a sentence in an interrogative form, addressed to someone in order to get information in reply.

Questions are an act of aggression—they are the verbal equivalent of rape! The woman who shouted this fought tears welling up in her eyes. Her companion was struck silent. His surprise and dismay were apparent. Mercifully, he did not speak. Others in the room were now focused on the pair. Silence embraced the passing moments. Finally, the woman felt composed enough to speak. Her voice was soft but trembling. "I'm sorry. It was just that you asked me five questions in a row and interrupted my answers with more questions!" The man showed his embarrassment. All he thought he was doing was carrying on the traditions of Socrates and Descartes. Injuring his colleague was not his intent. With his mumbled apology, the room filled with conversation, at first uneasy and then in a warm, rhythmic banter.

Bob says:

> *In my years of higher education, I often heard the statement, "The purpose of a good education is not to provide us with answers but rather to teach us to ask good questions." I bought into that statement for nearly a decade before it came to my attention that a question may be a logical pathway to reason, but may also be an aggression upon another's sense of well-being.*

Questions force disclosure. They demand explanation or justification.

Consider this. I was working in Crownpoint, New Mexico with children in a Bureau of Indian Affairs elementary school. I was using some instructional materials that my colleagues and I had developed in the field of environmental studies. They were what is called "inquiry based," at that time an instructional approach that was widely celebrated. I asked the students when it had last rained. A girl stood and said, "Last spring." I probed more, "What month did it rain?" The girl looked at me for a moment and then sat down. No one else stood. The room filled with awkward silence. I called on another of the students. He looked down at the surface of his desk and said nothing. I turned to another. She too dropped her eyes and looked at her desktop. I had no idea what was happening.

Later the Navajo teacher explained. When I first asked the question, a girl was perfectly willing to participate until I refused her answer. I was dumbfounded. "How did I refuse her answer?" I asked. The teacher dropped his eyes as well, and said, "When you discredited her answer by asking another question, the other students could not respond because it would have meant that her answer was not good. They could not discredit or embarrass their sister."

After some time with these children, I discovered how an act steeped in popular pedagogy and regarded as an excellent way to stimulate inquiry actually created an environment of discomfort and doubt. An approach that is designed to deepen understanding by building a web of meaning through questions instead reduced options and narrowed the opportunity for shared learning.

After returning from Crownpoint to Boulder, Colorado, where our project offices were located, I told my story. My colleagues and I began to look into the invisible effects of questioning on all students. In short order, we were able to determine that the majority of teachers with whom we worked used the interrogative more than 75 percent of the time.

This meant that students of all ages were being questioned most of the time they were being instructed. Moreover, homework, when it is given, is often a request to answer the questions at the end of chapters in the students' textbooks. Questions follow questions. Rare are the islands of relaxed discussion where ideas can flow and deepen in natural cycles.

Here are a few characteristics of questions.

"What" questions generally seek information. For example, "What time should we leave?" or "What are you going to wear?"

"Why" questions seek justification: "Why do we have to go so early?" "Why are you wearing that?" or "Why did you do that?" "What" questions tend to be the least intrusive. "Why" questions are the most intrusive and aggressive of questions. Think about the circumstances in which you hear the "why" question: "Why did you do that?" The question is designed to put the one who is supposed to answer on the defensive.

Think about "why" questions in public meetings. A concerned citizen will raise his or her hand to the elected officials and say, "Why are you taking this approach?" The already defensive public officials become even more defensive. The questioner may actually be looking for an objective response. However, "why" questions tend to be taken personally. People typically feel as if they have to justify themselves at a personal level in response.

"Why" questions are frequently carried in the baggage of emotion and feelings. "Why" often elevates insecurity, doubt and lack of confidence. "Why" is also a frequent weapon used by one person to put another on the defensive intentionally.

The cure for asking endless questions of others is to speak in the declarative. Instead of making the focus the person being asked the question, putting the statement in the form of a declarative begins the conversation with a positive disclosure. In contrast, the questioning approach demands someone else to disclose information. Questions are power plays. Statements level the playing field.

Activity: Practicing the Declarative

Stop asking questions at work for one hour.

Increase the time until you can avoid asking questions for a whole morning, afternoon or day.

Check your tendency to use questions to demonstrate courteous interest, seek information or put someone else on the defensive.

Check the number of times you feel put on the defensive by others who ask questions of you.

Talk to your family at dinner without asking a single question.

Go to a social event where you are meeting people for the first time and speak in the first person declarative throughout the evening. Compare the experience to those in which you say, "Hi. Live around here? Where do you work?"

Scapegoating

scape goat ism, noun. The act or practice of assigning blame or failure to someone or something.

In its classic form, scapegoating is what this definition indicates. We extend the definition. We see scapegoating as moving in two major directions. Scapegoating can be both assigning blame and failure and assigning credit and success to someone or something outside yourself. Scapegoating is an act of externalizing responsibility for what one experiences.

When Flip Wilson, a comic of the 1970s, was confronted by some outlandish act, he would always say, "The devil made me do it." Republicans scapegoat Democrats, and Democrats scapegoat Republicans. Political contests are endless demonstrations of scapegoating. Sibling rivalry frequently takes the form of scapegoating.

When I scapegoat, I externalize responsibility for what I am experiencing at a given moment. I give power to something outside myself. Bob tells this story.

> *Early in my career, I shared the timidity and insecurity of most students. I had developed the creative illusion of humility and reflexively deferred responsibility for what I had learned to my teachers. In other words, I was a good graduate student. I always footnoted whatever I said in order to properly credit those scholars who preceded me.*

I did that so much that, out of academic politeness, I confused what I knew with what my professors knew. At a party one evening, one of my most revered mentors, Richard Jones, strode up to me. He hugged me vigorously and said loudly, "Bob, I think we have both finally arrived." I was shocked and pleased. Richard said, "I have finally given up giving Freud credit for my ideas, and you have given up giving Bruner credit for yours!" I was embarrassed and puzzled. "I had never thought of it that way," I said. Responsible scholarship is one thing. Creating imaginary footnotes to avoid taking responsibility for one's own thoughts is a form of deceit. In a single moment, I learned that such a form of scapegoating is not a courtesy, but a lie.

Blaming and externalizing failure is often a lie. Another person making a mistake is not responsible for me choosing to follow him or her in that mistake. I am not innocent of responsibility when someone else makes an erroneous decision and I politely and courteously fail to bring it to his or her attention. We can recall many instances in which we witnessed people making wrongheaded decisions and failed to bring it to their attention. Failure resulted. We compounded the error by helping the people involved to create an excuse that ended up scapegoating the cause of the growing mess.

Racism is one of a variety of culturally instituted forms of scapegoating. It is supported by the shibboleths that have polite acceptance within the in-group and vicious consequences in the out-group

Scapegoating is the womb of discrimination. If we live in a culture that collectively scapegoats, we have the power to choose to reject such scapegoating or not. If I choose to put it aside, I must accept the responsibility to stand apart from much of my culture. I must accept being viewed with suspicion and disdain. Clearly, loneliness can be a companion to the intrinsic in a quest for civility in communities. In the long run, it is only through commitment to responsible harmony that we can achieve both personal and collective peace.

Activity: Scrapping Scapegoating

Make a list of scapegoating statements you have made in the past.

Make a list of things you feel are contributing to the failure of society and see how many are actually expressions of scape-goating.

Examine how scapegoating others affects your life.

Determine how many of your values rest on a bed of blaming others.

List how others scapegoat you. Reflect on how you feel when you are the recipient of scapegoating.

"Yes, but," and "Yes, and"

and, conjunction. used to connect. in addition to.
but, conjunction. on the contrary. except.

Bob tells this story:

> *I remember listening to a tape recording of the discourse that followed a panel discussion at a large international conference on learning. I had been a member of the panel and had participated in the discussion. At the time, I did not notice anything unusual. The discussion seemed informed and civil. When I listened later to the tape recording, I was struck by the use of the phrase "yes, but . . ." The phrase caught my attention because it was used by every speaker. I was amazed, as I counted the frequency of the use of the phrase, to hear it more than 30 times.*
>
> *Each speaker was a respected authority on learning. Each of us was taking our expertise in useful and important directions. Our collective vision was healing and transforming. In the process of discussion, however, each of us confronted the other with "yes, but . . ." as a transition from speaker to speaker. The result was that we sounded like we were taking exception to what one another had said. "But" means on the contrary and except. Our words had negative weight.*

We were communicating opposition and disagreement when our intent was to agree and support. "But" is a blow to a conversation. It is aggressive. It is designed to contradict, not support. Used reflexively, it separates rather than unifies.

Later, I talked with friends about "kicking the but habit." It is not as easy as we thought initially it would be. We tried substituting "yes, and ..." for "yes, but ..." "But" is so ingrained in common speech, we had to consciously lower our threshold of recognition. This same process must be used to get rid of any unwanted language patterns, or other unwanted habits. Once we developed a reflex to say, "yes, and ..." we noticed a heightened sense of cooperation.

"Yes, and" honors the perspective of the person who precedes you. It is more than a semantic trick. It is a palpable way to connect thoughts. "Yes, and . . ." accepts the previous thought and offers the possibility of extending it into new realms. "Yes, but ... " focuses on differences and disagreement. "Yes, and ... " focuses on similarities and agreement.

Having said all this, "yes, but ..." is perfectly appropriate when your purpose is to analyze a situation or emphasize points of difference. As with all of our recommendations about the power of words, the intent is to check the tendency. Check your tendency to say, "yes, but ..." Discern the times when you are interested in extending an idea rather than disagreeing with it.

Activity: Yes, and ...

Check your own emotion when you are greeted with these phrases in conversation:
"That is well and good, but ... "
"That simply is not true ... "
"I don't know where you get your information, but ..."
"I would not expect someone of your age/background/gender/experience to understand this, so ..."

Check your own tendency to use "but ..." in a conversation.

Write a note in your journal about those instances in which you seem to be most likely to interject "but."

PART FOUR
CONSCIOUSNESS

The true state of the material world is wholeness. If we are fragmented, we must blame it on ourselves.

David Bohm

The earth consists of a multitude, a near infinity of living species, all engaged in some kind of thought.

Lewis Thomas
The Fragile Species

Consciousness is what we pay attention to. We first heard this statement from Karl Pribram. This perspective leads to a powerful set of explorations that can help inform how we approach the process of achieving healthy communities. At the heart is consciousness.

Natural history has given us our bodies and brains, the physiology that we possess as humans. Cultural history has given us the abstractions that guide and hold us. Our first gestation as humans is in the womb of planetary consciousness; our second is in cultural consciousness.

Many years ago we introduced the concept of holonomy as a way to understand the forces that form human consciousness. Holonomy is born of two parents: *holos,* meaning whole or entire; and *nomy,* meaning science or systematic study. Holonomy is the science or systematic study of wholeness. The holonomic model that we propose, and did so more than 20 years ago, is a synthesis of various sources. Most notable for popularizing the substance and vision behind the holonomic model are Karl Pribram and David Bohm. Pribram's extensive experience as a neurosurgeon, neuroscientist and avid researcher has provided him with a wealth of insight that makes this model both theoretically and practically viable. Bohm, a physicist, has approached the issue from his studies of consciousness and physical systems. Throughout his explorations—whether in subatomic or cosmic dimensions—Bohm is a champion of unity and wholeness.

Pribram and Bohm have helped to lead us to the following. Minds are limited because the concept of mind is limited. Consciousness is narrow because we humans tend to narrow our attention when we listen to the closed-system thought that is characteristic of contemporary technological cultures.

Minds are limited

because the concept of mind is limited.

As Bob first observed in *Mind of Our Mother,* it is consciousness that limits the range of attention we honor in scanning the millions of contexts created by the brain-mind system. It is as though thoughts created by the brain-mind originate from endless cerebral meadows rich with flowers, butterflies and a myriad of other life forms. As we walk such meadows, our path is always narrow. What we become aware of is always limited and highly selective. It is consciousness that makes that selection. Again, as Pribram said, "consciousness is what we pay attention to." In the meadows of mind, we may one day gather a bouquet, another day observe insects, and yet another time map the paths we have taken. Only rarely do we experience the meadow in its entirety. For most of us, "paying attention" in consciousness is a process of reducing our vision. It is an act that involves a narrowing of perception.

Normal consciousness is what we pay attention to in a reflexive way. We think of consciousness as a ray of sunlight lancing through an opening in a cloudy sky and pouring out onto the Earth. This ray of finite width scans only a small portion of the landscape. So, too, consciousness scans only a small portion of our mindscape. Self-imposed habits in consciousness create a narrow range of options in terms of normal thought. Much more is available to us through the normal range of capacities we each can access. Consciousness is what we pay attention to. Consciousness opens the doors and windows that let the light of creativity illuminate our spirit, our practice, our hearts, and ultimately, the powers we have through our individual and collective energies to make the world a better place.

Change is a result of consciousness. Since all change is driven by consciousness in some form, we are interested in conscious choice—informed by an understanding of the characteristics of healthy communities—that will facilitate a directional move toward peace rather than destruction, prosperity rather than war, tranquility rather than terrorism.

If consciousness is what we each pay attention to, then creating a shift in consciousness is as simple as paying attention to different things. It is up to each of us, and begins within each one of us, while we connect through one another to all that is and ever will be. Consciousness is the dance of the spirit, the song that connects, the hope for the future.

We return to natural systems for perspective. It is only in nature that the most persistent of open systems prevail. We need to re-ground ourselves in the ways of wild ecologies in order to gain the kind of perspective that will enliven our capacities to choose forms of consciousness that will heal the strife that exists within the human communities of the world. It is nature that will guide us to the kind of realistic, dynamic equilibrium that we need in order to heal the rifts between culture and nature.

We hold the view that consciousness is universal. Consistent with the worldviews of Native American traditions, and those of contemporary scientists such as Lewis Thomas and Lynn Margulis, we believe that there is consciousness in all life.

Consciousness is the dance of the spirit,
the song that connects,
the hope for the future.
It is nature that will guide us to the kind of realistic, dynamic equilibrium that we need in order to heal the rifts between culture and nature.

We believe that natural consciousness and cultural consciousness must be brought together in dynamic balance and harmony, integrated and whole. We are out of balance, with too much emphasis on the cultural, and too little on the natural ecologies of consciousness. Putting them back into balance is the hope for the future, the promise of community, the way of "coming home."

It is up to each of us—and then each of us is part of, and contributes to, the whole. We have choices to make and work to do. The future of life on Earth, and the quality of that life, depends on a critical mass of people using their personal creativity and their conscious commitment to create a world of peace in the 21st century.

Activity: Committing to Community

Take a deep breath. If you've just finished this book (for the first time, since we encourage you to read and interact with it as a conversation over time), take a few moments to reflect. In your journal, write a haiku, bumper sticker or short poem to represent what you most want to change in your own life in order to be an even more effective contributor to the health of communities, now and in the future. Illustrate it any way that feels appropriate to you—by putting images around it, embedding it in a digital photo of your own, writing it on a natural piece of parchment that you have made yourself, or whatever other means comes to mind.

Imagine what you want to accomplish in the next year, five years, ten years. Imagine what you want a peaceful, healthy and sustainable future to look like. Write a description of that healthy future. Refer to it in one year, five years, ten years. Save it for a generation to follow.

Get involved. Do what you can every day to take care of yourself and those you love, to enrich and help to foster collaboration in every setting in which you live, learn, play and work, and to give to the Earth itself. Remember, "Earth Is Home to Us All—Share It Responsibly."

Acknowledgements

It is a privilege to honor some of the many people who have inspired, taught, befriended, and mentored us in our lives. It is with trepidation that we make any attempt to do so—with concern for those we will inadvertently omit and recognition that there are far more who have helped to guide us than space will allow us to name. We offer our apologies in advance to those we do not acknowledge.

We begin with family—parents, grandparents, great-grandparents, aunts, uncles and cousins, all of whom have brought us enduring gifts, and, so close to our hearts and engaged in so many of the same pursuits as his parents, our son, Stician Marin Samples.

We have had the good fortune to work with, learn from, collaborate and share friendship with an extraordinary number of individuals—some famous, some not, and all important to us.

In the early years of Bob's career, among those were Jerome Bruner, Richard Jones, and Frances and David Hawkins. Early for Cheryl were Sara Moss Phillips, Mary Guptill Warren, Martha McGeorge Hunter, Charles Billings and Irving Morrissett.

Through the years, others appeared—Rosemarie and Bill Hammond, Rosemary and Dick Barnhart, Judy and David Kennedy, Katie and Cliff Hamilton, Pat and Jake Nice, Margie and Ned Herrmann, Suzie and Nick Helburn, Jo and Steve Wilson, Jan Rensel and Alan Howard, Ed and Judy Dawson, Della and Milton McClaren, Cliff Knapp and Jan Woodhouse, Kerry Baldwin and Tina Allen, Annie and Frank Watson, Pat McQuown, Gail and Harley Lyons, Robin and Phil Ecklund, Carol Bylsma, Joanna Prukop, Kimberley Sweet, Joseph Hesbrook, Lyn Fleming, Susan and George Otero, Peter Corcoran, Tony Angell, Larry Littlebird, Laura Sanderford and Ron Schultz, Howard Sherman, Brad Peterson, Allan Savory, Stephen Kellert, Jonas Salk, and Mary Catherine Bateson.

Beginning in the late 1970s, the Windstar years began, starting with the Reverend David Randle introducing Bob to Tom Crum, and then both of us to John Denver, saying, "You have a lot in common." That was the beginning of an enduring friendship of shared interests in spirit, the environment, community, and the world of ideas. Of the many with whom we shared Windstar's vision and "Choices for a Healthy Future," some with whom our connection has been the deepest are John Denver, Ann and Rolland Smith, Cathy and Tom Crum, Joan and Jim Leary, Dave Randle, Jeanie Tomlinson, Carmen Volcansek, Micki and Dan McCormick, Jean Michel-Cousteau, Hunter and Amory Lovins, Jean Houston, Noel Brown, Sally Ranney, Steve Conger, Dorothy and Hal Thau, Rick Chappell, Hal Bidlack, Leah and Jay Hair and Buckminster Fuller—and, in recent years, Marge and Doug MacDonald, Sue DiCicco, and Ron Deutchendorf.

We met Beth and Charles Miller at the home of John Denver in the late 1980s, and that was the beginning of the Sol y Sombra years. While we shared the Windstar connection, serving as board members and advisors, Sol y Sombra added a dimension as an extraordinary gathering place. For the 13 years that Beth and Charles opened the gates of their Santa Fe home to people throughout the world, those who arrived and stayed awhile enriched one another and all of us who gathered. Our interests and conversations ranged from politics to world peace, water conservation to world affairs, the arts to the emerging science of complex adaptive systems. Of the many who were Beth's and Charles' guests, among those with whom we again connected most deeply as friends and students of the world of ideas and good works are Carol Anthony, Brian Arthur, Joe Jaworski, Arturo Madrid, Governor Ann Richards, John Bradshaw, Mary and Ben Greig, Sara Jane Eads, Nancy "Fred" Mims, Stuart Kauffmann, Rodger Boyd, Governor Bill and Barbara Richardson, Lee and Stewart Udall and Murray Gell-Mann. Others who inspired and informed our thinking were Bill Moyers, the Dalai Lama, Angela Glover Blackwell, and Marian Wright Edelman.

With Beth and Charles Miller, we founded the Center for the Study of Community, and developed the Community Building Institute. Among the board, faculty, advisors, participants and friends who made significant contributions through those years are Greg Curtis, Steve Feinberg and Susan Foote, Owen Lopez, Betty Sue Flowers, Mary Beth Rogers, Dan Kemmis, Carl Moore, Rosemary Romero, Greg Cajete, Tyler Norris, Dee Hock, and John Gardner. Of the participants—those leaders who are willing learners—there are too many to name. Among them are Congressman Tom Udall, Tom Thomason, Ed Mazria, Toby Herzlich, Nancy Wirth and Miguel Grunstein.

In recent years, our lives have been enriched by the addition of Catherine A. Allen, John Burke, Susan Munroe and Terry Smith, Teresa Lindsey and Joe Wesselkamper, and Gary Roboff.

For nearly two decades, Janet Rasmussen and her daughters have been an important part of our extended family. The many ways in which Janet personally and professionally contributes to our lives are incalculable. We are deeply grateful.

Susanna Space and Melissa Latham-Stevens provided editorial and design assistance for *Coming Home,* respectively. They have, in different ways, helped us to bring grace to these pages.

We offer our special gratitude to Bradley Winch, Bob's publisher and friend for many years. His and Cathy Winch's loving support are reflected throughout these pages.

We thank each of these generous people. Their support, encouragement, love and friendship help us to feel "at home" wherever we are.

RESOURCES WE RECOMMEND

Abrashoff, Captain D. Michael. *It's Your Ship*. New York: Warner Books, 2002.

Augros, Robert and George Stanciu. *The New Biology: Discovering the Wisdom in Nature*. Boston: Shambhala, 1988.

Bateson, Gregory. *Mind and Nature: A Necessary Unity*. New York: E.P. Dutton, 1979.

Bateson, Gregory. *Steps to an Ecology of Mind*. New York: Ballantine Books, 1972.

Bateson, Gregory and Mary Catherine Bateson. *Angels Fear: Towards an Epistemology of the Sacred*. New York: Macmillan Publishing Company, 1987.

Bateson, Mary Catherine. *Full Circles, Overlapping Lives: Culture and Generation in Transition*. New York: Random House, Inc., 2000.

Bateson, Mary Catherine. *Our Own Metaphor: A Personal Account of a Conference on the Effects of Conscious Purpose on Human Adaptation*. Washington, DC: Smithsonian Institution Press, 1991. (First Edition, Knopf, 1972)

Bateson, Mary Catherine. *Peripheral Visions: Learning Along the Way*. New York: HarperCollins Publishers, Inc., 1994.

Beck, Don Edward and Christopher C. Cowan. *Spiral Dynamics: Mastering Values, Leadership and Change*. Malden, Mass.: Blackwell Publishers Inc., 1996.

Brown, John Seely and Paul Duguid. *The Social Life of Information*. Boston: Harvard Business School Press, 2000.

Bruner, Jerome S. *On Knowing: Essays for the Left Hand*. New York: Atheneum, 1973.

Bryan, Mark, Julia Cameron and Catherine A. Allen. *The Artist's Way at Work*. New York: William Morrow and Company, 1998.

Cajete, Gregory. *Native Science: Natural Laws of Interdependence*. Santa Fe: Clear Light Publishers, 2000.

Daly, Herman E. and John B. Cobb, Jr. *For the Common Good: Redirecting the Economy Toward Community, the Environment, and a Sustainable Future.* Boston: Beacon Press, 1989.

Ellis, Dave. *Falling Awake: Creating the Life of Your Dreams.* Rapid City, S.D.: Breakthrough Enterprises, Inc., 2002.

Gardner, John W. *On Leadership.* New York: Macmillan, Inc., 1990.

Hawken, Paul, Amory Lovins and L. Hunter Lovins. *Natural Capitalism: Creating the Next Industrial Revolution.* Boston: Little, Brown and Company, 1999.

Hock, Dee. *Birth of the Chaordic Age.* San Francisco: Berrett-Koehler Publishers, Inc., 1999.

Jantsch, Erich. *The Self-Organizing Universe: Scientific and Human Implications of the Emerging Paradigm of Evolution.* Oxford: Pergamon Press, 1980.

Kanter, Rosabeth Moss. *Evolve! Succeeding in the Digital Culture of Tomorrow.* Boston: Harvard Business School Press, 2001.

Keller, Ed and John Berry. *The Influentials.* New York: Simon and Schuster, Inc., 2003.

Kellert, Stephen R. and Edward O. Wilson (Editors). *The Biophilia Hypothesis.* Washington DC: Island Press, 1993.

Kemmis, Daniel. *Community and the Politics of Place.* Norman, Okla.: University of Oklahoma Press, 1990.

Kemmis, Daniel. *The Good City and the Good Life: Renewing the Sense of Community.* Boston: Houghton Mifflin Company, 1995.

Putnam, Robert D. *Bowling Alone: The Collapse and Revival of American Community.* New York: Simon and Schuster, 2000.

Putnam, Robert D., Lewis M. Feldstein, with Don Cohen. *Better Together: Restoring the American Community.* New York: Simon and Schuster, 2003.

Rosen, Robert H. *The Healthy Company.* New York: Jeremy P. Tarcher/Perigree, 1991.

Roszak, Theodore. *The Making of a Counterculture.* Garden City, NY: Doubleday & Company, Inc., 1968, 1969.

Salk, Jonas. *Anatomy of Reality: Merging of Intuition and Reason. New York:* Columbia University Press, 1983.

Samples, Bob and Bob Wohlford. *Opening: A Primer for Self Actualization.* Menlo Park: Addison Wesley, 1973.

Samples, Bob, Cheryl Charles and Dick Barnhart. *The WholeSchool Book: Teaching and Learning Late in the 20th Century.* Menlo Park: Addison Wesley, 1977.

Samples, Bob. *Mind of Our Mother.* Menlo Park: Addison Wesley, 1981.

Samples, Bob. *Open Mind, Whole Mind.* Rolling Hills Estates, Calif.: Jalmar Press, 1999.

Samples, Bob. *The Metaphoric Mind: A Celebration of Creative Consciousness.* Rolling Hills Estates, Calif.: Jalmar Press, 1993. (First Edition, Addison Wesley, 1976)

Saul, John Ralston. *The Unconscious Civilization.* Concord, Ontario: House of Anansi Press Limited, 1995.

Sherman, Howard and Ron Schultz. *Open Boundaries: Creating Business Innovation Through Complexity.* Reading: Perseus Books, 1998.

Skolimowski, Henryk. *The Participatory Mind: A New Theory of Knowledge and of the Universe.* New York: Penguin Books, 1994.

Takaki, Ronald. *A Different Mirror: A History of Multicultural America.* New York: Little, Brown and Company, 1993.

Thomas, Lewis. *The Fragile Species.* New York: Macmillan Publishing Company, 1992.

Thomas, Lewis. *The Lives of a Cell: Notes of a Biology Watcher.* New York: Bantam Books, Inc., 1974.

Wirzba, Norman (Editor). *The Art of the Common Place: The Agrarian Essays of Wendell Berry.* Washington, DC: Counterpoint, 2002.

About the Authors
Cheryl Charles and Bob Samples

Photo by Steve Yadzinski

Te authors have spent the last 30 years together working on ways to improve the quality of life for learners of all ages. They began their careers as educators, met and married, and raised a son. Along the way, they each were directors of national level education programs. They have pioneered work to foster cooperation and collaborative problem solving in settings as diverse as homes, schools, businesses, and municipalities. They have always believed in each person's capacity to learn, be creative, exercise leadership and participate in the process of protecting the civic health of this Nation's communities. They have a deep conservation ethic and commitment to the health of natural systems. Drawing on all these interests and experiences, they have created *Coming Home*.

Cheryl Charles has served as National Director of the widely used K-12 environment education programs, Project Learning Tree and Project WILD. She served as Chair of the Board of John Denver's Windstar Foundation, President of the Windstar Land Conservancy, and co-founded a think tank to focus on issues facing communities. In the past ten years, she has expanded her scope to bring collaborative skills to the competitive environment of the financial services industry. Recipient of numerous awards for her leadership, she received her Ph.D. from the University of Washington.

Bob Samples is author of numerous books and films, including the classics, *The Metaphoric Mind, Open Mind/Whole Mind*, and *Opening: A Primer for Self Actualization*. Widely sought as a keynote speaker and lecturer, his intellect, insights and humor have graced many stages through the years. Trained as a natural scientist, his work for the past three decades has focused on enhancing creativity, respecting learners, and applying natural systems concepts to human affairs. Respected for his innovation and leadership, Bob served for many years as national director of National Science Foundation funded educational projects. Bob received his Masters of Education from the University of Colorado in Boulder.